THE GREAT
VISIONS
OF ELLEN G. WHITE

Volume 1

Other Books by Roger Coon

A Gift of Light (1983)

Ellen G. White and Vegetarianism: Did She Practice What She Preached? (1986)

Heralds of New Light: Another Prophet to the Remnant? (1987)

"Look a Little Higher" (1990)

THE GREAT
VISIONS
OF ELLEN G. WHITE

Volume 1

Roger W. Coon

REVIEW AND HERALD® PUBLISHING ASSOCIATION
HAGERSTOWN, MD 21740

This book was
Edited by Raymond H. Woolsey
Designed by Bill Kirstein
Cover design by Helcio Deslandes
Cover illustration by Harry Anderson
Type set: 11/12 Garamond Book

PRINTED IN U.S.A.

95 94 93 92 91   10 9 8 7 6 5 4 3 2 1

Library of Congress Cataloging in Publication Data

Coon, Roger W.
    The great visions of Ellen G. White / Roger W. Coon.
        p.   cm.
    Includes bibliographical references.
        1. White, Ellen Gould Harmon, 1827-1915. 2. Visions—History,
I. Title.
BX6193.W5C67   1992
286.7—dc20   92-11514
                                                        CIP

ISBN 0-8280-0636-9 (v. 1)

DEDICATION

To
Robert W. Olson, Th.D.,
Associate Secretary (1974-78) and Secretary (1978-90),
Ellen G. White Estate,
my
friend, colleague, counselor,
elder brother in the upward walk,
imitator of Jesus,
and, truly,
the epitome of Ellen White's ideal:
"a loving and lovable Christian."

Acknowledgments

"Pay each one his due," the apostle Paul reminded the Christians of Rome nearly two millennia ago: "taxes to whom taxes are due; toll to whom toll is due; respect and honor to everyone who deserves them" (Rom. 13:7, NAB).

Such is not only an ethical Christian obligation, but a very special privilege as well, especially for writers. For as John Donne wrote in the seventeenth century, "no man is an island, entire of itself "; and as Tennyson had his character Ulysses confess in the nineteenth century, "I am a part of all that I have met."

Very rarely is a book the product of one man's or of one woman's creativity. Appreciation as well as credit is due especially to

—the trustees of the Ellen G. White Estate, Inc., and more particularly to its president and chairman, Kenneth H. Wood, and to the two executive secretaries whose tenure overlapped the development of the manuscript—Robert W. Olson and Paul A. Gordon—for providing both the time and encouragement for the development of this project.

—fellow colleagues in the White Estate, who critically read various chapters in manuscript form, and who offered most helpful suggestions regarding potential sources and manuscript improvement. (Mistakes, errors, and evidence of poor reasoning or judgment should not, however, be chargeable to them!)

—secretaries Dolores Wisbey, Lois Covarubbias, and Carol Pack, who worked their computer magic in word processing and formatting of materials for various successive reincarnations in print.

—General Conference graphics designer Irv Heller, for his helpful sketch illustrating Ellen White's "platform" vision in chapter 3.

—D. A. Delafield, who provided, in the pilot presentation of Testimony Countdown III, a splendid vehicle for field-testing ideas and materials in a live audience situation at the Takoma Park (Maryland) Seventh-day Adventist Church on 10 Wednesday evenings, January 16 through March 20, 1991.

—printing craftsman Lee Belcher and his General Conference Duplication Services colleagues, who skillfully, promptly, and faithfully prepared and printed the 10 chapters of this book week by week as individual audience handouts for those attending Testimony Countdown III over a period of nearly three months.

—Raymond H. Woolsey, who took time from administrative responsibilities as vice president for book editorial at the Review and Herald to edit this manuscript.

—and to my wife, Irene, who settled for less husband than was her due, during the long and lonely hours of writing, rewriting, and final editing, often between 2:00 and 6:00 a.m., during weekends, and over holidays.

And so to all such, a hearty and fervent "Thank you!"

Contents

Abbreviations

AA	*The Acts of the Apostles*
AH	*The Adventist Home*
1BC	*The Seventh-day Adventist Bible Commentary*, vol. 1 (2BC, etc., for vols. 2-7)
1Bio	Arthur L. White, *Ellen G. White*, vol. 1 (2Bio, etc., for vols. 2-6)
CD	*Counsels on Diet and Foods*
CH	*Counsels on Health*
CM	*Colporteur Ministry*
COL	*Christ's Object Lessons*
CS	*Counsels on Stewardship*
CT	*Counsels to Parents and Teachers*
CW	*Counsels to Writers and Editors*
DA	*The Desire of Ages*
DF	Ellen G. White Estate Document File
Ed	*Education*
Ev	*Evangelism*
EW	*Early Writings*
GC	*The Great Controversy*
GCB	*General Conference Bulletin*
GSAM	J. N. Loughborough, *The Great Second Advent Movement*
1Index	*Comprehensive Index to the Writings of Ellen G. White*, vol. 1 (2Index, etc., for vols. 2, 3)
Letter	Ellen G. White letter
LHU	*Lift Him Up*
LS	*Life Sketches*
1MCP	*Mind, Character, and Personality*, vol. 1 (2MCP for vol. 2)
MH	*The Ministry of Healing*
MLT	*My Life Today*
MM	*Medical Ministry*
1MR	*Ellen G. White Manuscript Releases,* vol. 1 (2MR, etc., for successive volumes)
Ms	Ellen G. White manuscript
PK	*Prophets and Kings*
PP	*Patriarchs and Prophets*
RH	*Review and Herald*
RPSDA	J. N. Loughborough, *Rise and Progress of Seventh-day Adventists*
SC	*Steps to Christ*
SD	*Sons and Daughters of God*
SDAE	*Seventh-day Adventist Encyclopedia* (1976)
1SG	*Spiritual Gifts*, vol. 1 (2SG, etc., for vols. 2-4)
1SM	*Selected Messages*, book 1 (2SM, etc., for books 2, 3)
1SP	*The Spirit of Prophecy,* vol. 1 (2SP, etc., for vols. 2-4)
ST	*Signs of the Times*
1T	*Testimonies*, vol. 1 (2T, etc., for vols. 2-9)
Te	*Temperance*
TM	*Testimonies to Ministers*
UL	*The Upward Look*
WM	*Welfare Ministry*

How This Book Came to Be

Author's Introduction

The Seventh-day Adventist Church was cofounded by James and Ellen White and Joseph Bates at Battle Creek, Michigan, in 1860. But its origins stretch back three decades earlier to the 1830s, when a Baptist farmer-turned-preacher, William Miller, began to preach the imminent return of Jesus Christ to this earth. Miller mistakenly agreed with a few other contemporary expositors of Bible time prophecies that the date for that event would be October 22, 1844.

Some six or seven weeks after the ensuing "Great Disappointment," on a now unknown day in December, 1844, a 17-year-old maiden, Ellen Harmon (later Mrs. James White), received a vision. It was the first of hundreds of prophetic dreams and visions, spanning a period of seven decades. Seventh-day Adventists quickly came to view them as of divine origin.

During this remarkably fecund 70-year ministry to her church, some 25 million words would issue forth from the pen of Ellen White. Even in death she would attain to literary distinction, for she has been constituted as (1) one of the most translated writers in the entire history of literature (in 1991 her treatise on practical Christian living, *Steps to Christ,* was available in 137 languages); (2) the most translated *woman* writer of all time; and (3) the most translated *American* writer of either sex.

Adventists have held since earliest times that her writings were inspired by the Holy Spirit in the same manner—and to the same degree—as those of the 40-plus writers of the Bible. Yet they assiduously refrain from making of them either a substitute Bible or an addition to the sacred canon of Scripture.

Rather, the church sees Mrs. White in a role analogous to that of the eight men mentioned in the Old Testament who were acknowledged to be divinely inspired *literary* prophets—Jasher, Gad, Nathan, Ahijah the Shilonite, Shemaiah, Iddo, Jehu, and Elijah—yet whose writings never appeared in the Bible.

While not making belief in Mrs. White's fascinating gift of prophetic inspiration a test of church membership, Adventists still have strongly upheld her unique role in their heritage. And entire courses dealing with her life, ministry, writings, and pronounce-

11

ments have been and are being taught in Seventh-day Adventist colleges and universities on all six continents.

The textbook for the undergraduate introductory course in Seventh-day Adventist prophetic guidance, since 1955, has been T. Housel Jemison's *A Prophet Among You*. It has done yeoman service for some 35 years; but eventually it has become viewed as more and more out of date (through no fault of the author's) vis-à-vis the changing issues and needs within and without the church.

On December 14, 1989, the trustees of the Ellen G. White Estate at Seventh-day Adventist world church headquarters concurred with the request of the Pacific Press Publishing Association of Boise, Idaho, that I be assigned the task of preparing a replacement textbook. Jemison's work had 24 chapters, with some 600 pages of text; mine, now in progress, will have perhaps 28 chapters, and approximately 650 pages of text.

Despite the size of this editorial undertaking, it quickly became clear that several other works would also have to be written to round out the intention of the publisher and of the White Estate.

Two parallel series of volumes, giving background readings of historical and theological materials, would be needed to support the textbook: *The Great Visions of Ellen G. White* (of which this book is volume 1), and *The Great Messages of Ellen G. White* (as yet to be written) were among such.

A cursory look at this volume's table of contents may bring disappointment to some readers whose favorite vision story is left untold. I hope that volume 2 in this series will—at least in part—rectify that deficiency.

And the reader may well inquire: Why these stories, instead of some others equally appropriate to the theme? By what yardstick were these particular vision stories selected for inclusion in this book?

There were at least six criteria that informed and guided the selection process at every stage of development—and it is quickly conceded that these might well have led another researcher into quite different paths. I asked myself:

1. Does this vision story illustrate some aspect or facet of that marvelous and mysterious process to which theologians often refer when they speak of "inspiration" and "revelation," thereby enlarging our understanding of how this fascinating process came to work in practical day-to-day terms?

2. Does this vision story help to demonstrate how God used this

precious gift of the Holy Spirit in Adventism's historical past to shape the growth and development of our church?

3. Does this vision story help us to understand more fully—and, therefore, appreciate more—a major doctrine of our church, enabling us to see more clearly the precise nature of Ellen White's role in regard to her relationship and contribution to that doctrine?

4. Does this vision story possess a large quotient of human-interest factors that would better enable us to understand the humanity of this prophet called of God (as well as that of those who preceded her)?

5. Does this vision story help to establish and confirm our appreciation for, and confidence in, God, His love for our church, and His special gift to our people?

6. Does this vision story contribute—as, indeed, all of Mrs. White's ministry was intended to contribute—to our being better Christians? And does it also help us to prepare for the soon return of our Lord?

Each vision story in this volume (and in those to follow in this series) meets at least one of the above criteria. And each is presented here with a most fervent prayer that the examination of (and thoughtful personal reflection upon) each of these remarkable, dramatic incidents in our collective past will bring to you, the reader, as rich a spiritual blessing in the perusal as I have received in researching and writing them.

Roger W. Coon
Highland, Maryland

CHAPTER 1

THE FIRST VISION

"The Path"

December 1844

AT Christ's first miracle, when He turned water into unfermented wine [1] at Cana, the governor of the wedding feast declared that his host had kept the best for the last (John 2:10). Just so, in the year 1844, Jesus again seems to have saved His "best"—a renewed bestowal of the Holy Spirit's gift of prophetic utterance—for the last month of that year.

Just as a jewel is most brilliant in its proper setting, so this climactic act of Providence, to be most fully appreciated, must be viewed in the greater light of its immediate historical context.

What a pivotal year was 1844!

The eleventh president of the United States was to be chosen on Election Day in late autumn. Earlier in the year, the political campaign between Democrat James K. Polk and Whig Henry Clay was already hot when it was joined by a third contender, Joseph Smith, founder of the Church of Jesus Christ of Latter-day Saints and also of the Mormon colony in Nauvoo, Illinois.

Smith's candidacy was short-lived, however. The thought of a polygamist in the White House scandalized many, even on the frontier. A newspaper editor who strongly dissented in print suffered vengeance by fire from the Sons of Dan, vigilante night riders. Joseph Smith and his brother Hyrum were arrested, then tragically assassinated, defenseless in their jail cell at Carthage, Illinois, on June 27. [2] But there was more to come.

The summer of 1844 saw religious excitement vie with political for the attention of the masses. For this was the year that Jesus was supposed to return to earth from heaven, according to the preaching over the past 13 years by farmer-turned-Baptist evangelist, William Miller. Miller, it must be pointed out, never prescribed a precise date; but that deficiency was conveniently supplied at an Exeter, New Hampshire, camp meeting (which began August 11), by one Samuel Sheffield Snow.

Snow breathlessly rode into camp and electrified the congregation (and, subsequently, the eastern United States) by announcing his calculation that this history-shattering event would take place on October 22 of that very year, a scant three months later! [3]

Thus Snow unwittingly set the Millerites up for the "Great Disappointment," which began at 12:01 a.m. on October 23, after Jesus failed to appear as scheduled. Two weeks later, on November 5, Henry Clay endured his own personal "great disappointment" when he went down to defeat at the hands of American voters in his fourth (of five) unsuccessful attempts to win the U.S. presidency.

Finally, in the final month of that year, God acted!

The exact day in December is lost to history, as is also the exact street address in Portland, Maine, where Elizabeth Haines resided. [4] But what happened in her home would never be forgotten by any of the five women who gathered for family devotions to pray for guidance and a divine explanation of the meaning of their disappointment.

According to an eyewitness, several had already prayed when a young woman who had just celebrated her seventeenth birthday (on November 26) began to address the Lord in a hoarse whisper. Although it was not an exciting occasion, yet suddenly, in a movement surely as dramatic as was Pentecost itself, the Holy Spirit came into that dwelling and took physical possession of the petitioner. And Joel 2:28-32 found another fulfillment when this modern "handmaid" lost consciousness of her immediate surroundings, "the power of God came upon me," and "I was wrapped in a vision of God's glory." [5]

Thus Ellen Harmon, later to become Mrs. James White (on August 30, 1846), was inaugurated as God's newest prophet to His people.

Improbable Candidate for Prophet

Surely heaven's candidate was the most improbable in the entire history of prophets. Adventism's first historian, J. N. Loughborough, was probably the first to characterize her in print as the "weakest of the weak"—but he claims that this title did not originate with him. It was supplied by the angel who came to Hazen Foss in the latter's third vision in 1844, in which the hapless Foss was released from any further prophetic commission. [6]

Ellen Harmon had been a near-total invalid for the previous eight years because of a tragic rock-throwing incident. The accident had left her physically disfigured, her central nervous system shattered, and her formal education permanently terminated in the third (or, possibly, fourth) grade of elementary school. Hers was virtually a medical "basket case."

One physician observed that her right lung was "decayed," her left lung was "considerably diseased," and her heart action impaired. His diagnosis: "dropsical consumption" (a form of tuberculosis); his prognosis: at best her life expectancy was very short, at worst she was "liable to drop away at any time."

In order to breathe at night Ellen had to be propped up into a near-sitting position, and frequent coughing spasms and lung hemorrhages had almost totally sapped her physical strength. [7]

Certainly "weakest of the weak" was an apt description of God's third choice [8] for the office of prophet in the first half of the decade of the 1840s!

In 1840 Ellen White had been converted to the doctrine of Christ's imminent return under the preaching of William Miller himself; thus, on October 23, 1844, she, along with some 50,000 other followers of Miller, became one of the "Disappointed."

Within the next several years the discouraged (who did not remain in their earlier church affiliation) would sort themselves out into as many as four categories: (1) those who—whether from personal embarrassment, frustration, anger at God, or perhaps even misguided revenge—would give up *all* religious experience; (2) a lunatic fringe who veered off into tangents of successive date-settings, as well as other fanatical aberrations and excesses; (3) Sundaykeeping "Adventists" who continued to observe the first day of the week and to believe the Advent near, principally the Advent Christian Church; and (4) a very small group (initially only a few dozen) who would begin to coalesce around the leadership of James and Ellen White and Joseph Bates, accept the Saturday Sabbath of the

Seventh Day Baptists, and (in 1860-1863) form the Seventh-day Adventist denomination.

Doubtless none of those five women on that historic December day in 1844 grasped the reality that Ellen Harmon was actually witnessing the first of hundreds of divine visions and prophetic dreams, over a period of 70 years. Relating those visions and enunciating their import would result in a torrent of some 25 million words that, by 1992, would be published in 137 languages around the globe!

(Even in death Ellen White would attain to a certain literary distinction, for today she is (1) one of the most translated authors in the entire history of literature, (2) the most translated woman writer, and (3) the most-translated American writer of either sex!) [9]

The First Vision Described

Ellen herself, writing about this first vision, described it in these words:

"While I was praying at the family altar, the Holy Ghost fell upon me, and I seemed to be rising higher and higher, far above the dark world. I turned to look for the Advent people in the world, but could not find them, when a voice said to me, "look again, and look a little higher." At this I raised my eyes, and saw a straight and narrow path, cast up high above the world. On this path the Advent people were traveling to the city [New Jerusalem], which was at the farther end of the path.

"They had a bright light set up behind them at the beginning of the path, which an angel told me was the midnight cry. This light shone all along the path and gave light for their feet so that they might not stumble. If they kept their eyes fixed on Jesus, who was just before them, leading them to the city, they were safe. But soon some grew weary, and said the city was a great way off, and they expected to have entered it before. Then Jesus would encourage them by raising His glorious right arm, and from His arm came a light which waved over the Advent band, and they shouted, 'Alleluia.'

"Others rashly denied the light behind them and said that it was not God that had led them out so far. The light behind them went out, leaving their feet in perfect darkness, and they stumbled and lost sight of the mark and of Jesus, and fell off the path down into the dark and wicked world below." [10]

God's Purpose in 1844

Note that this first vision was given to a 17-year-old Sundaykeeping pork eater—and it said nothing about either the right day upon which Christians should worship God, or of the desirability of a vegetarian diet!

Rather, God's purpose in this first vision seems to have been to bring comfort and assurance to a dispirited band of Christians who had literally staked their all upon a sincere conviction. They had "put their money where their mouth was," but, through no fault of their own, they had been shaken and shattered, nearly as badly as were Christ's 11 surviving disciples on the day of His crucifixion.

The vision gave them *comfort* in knowing that God had directed them to the present day in their theological understanding, and that He had not deserted them in the bitter aftermath of October 22. It gave them *assurance* that if they remained faithful to God, each of them would ultimately find his or her way into the heavenly city, and that their present theological difficulties would be made plain—in God's own way and time, of course.

God's Message Today

And what is God's message for us today who still continue to "look for" (Heb. 9:28) and to "love" (2 Tim. 4:8) His appearing?

The dominant scene of this first vision was of a group of people traveling toward a city on "a straight and narrow path, cast high up above the world." Instinctively one's thoughts go to Christ's sermon on the mount and His metaphor of a "narrow way," little traveled, that leads to eternal life, and a "broad way," much traveled, that leads to destruction (Matt. 7:13, 14). One somehow senses, upon reflection, that these are not in reality two separate roads, but rather one road—the "road of life"—with two opposite destinations.

The apostle Paul seems especially to have been struck by this metaphor. In at least six of his Epistles [11] he picks up on this idea of the Christian "walk." The Christian is not simply out walking aimlessly for the lack of something more important to do; rather he walks purposefully, toward a predetermined goal.

(In a parallel metaphor, that of an athlete engaged in a foot race, Paul sees the Christian as "running" along an established course, with a well-defined goal at the end. But Paul supplies this twist: *everyone* can win this prize, not just the contestant who happens to cross the finish line first with his torch still burning!) [12]

And the lessons for us today in all of this?

1. We are all on the "road of life," which has two—and only two—destinations. Actually we are born headed in the downward direction; but Christ intercepts us with the gospel and invites us to "convert" (literally, "turn around") and instead to head uphill toward His city. Comparatively few are willing to make the transition and the transit.

2. Ever since the three temptations of Christ in the wilderness, on appetite, pride, and surrender to "captivating scenes of this world," Satan's strategy for subversion of Christians continues "in every possible way . . . to make the broad road attractive and the narrow road grievous, humiliating, and objectionable." [13]

3. Each must walk for himself; none can be carried by another.

4. In the context of river travel, it is more difficult and arduous to row upstream than to drift downstream; we either climb up the narrow way or slide down the broad.

5. The "road of life" has two ditches, one on either side. Both are to be avoided, whether that of ultraliberalism on the one hand, or that of archconservatism on the other. The more narrow the road, the more difficult (and more important) it is, and the more concentration is required, to stay in the middle.

This last thought would continue to absorb the attention of the prophet, becoming a recurring theme in her writings.

The Importance of Balance

The writings of Ellen White are replete with contrasting categories: "bigotry," "extremism," "fanaticism," "narrowness," "smallness," and "tangent," on the one hand; and "balance," "moderation," "equilibrium," and "common sense" on the other.

In the area of dress she cautioned: "Shun extremes." [14] "There is a medium position in these things. Oh, that we all might wisely find that position and keep it." [15]

In the area of diet, she repeatedly urged, "Take the middle path, avoiding all extremes." [16]

In the area of educational theory and practice she pleaded: "God wants us all to have common sense, and He wants us to reason from common sense." [17]

Ellen White viewed many a vice as being a virtue that has been carried to an unwarranted extreme: "It is carrying that which is lawful to excess that makes it a grievous sin." [18] Satan recognized that if he can get Christians into either the right-hand or the left-hand ditch of the road to heaven, they will make no forward advancement. Therefore, he seeks to change the metaphor—to get Christians into the "ice of indifference" or the "fire of fanaticism." [19] Either will suit his purpose.

And her lament for the church of her day is equally applicable to our own:

"There is a class of people who are always ready to go off on some tangent, who want to catch up something strange and wonderful and new." [20]

Her reasons for opposing extremists and urging moderate views are practical and not far to seek:

1. They bring the church into "disrepute"; a few can discredit the entire body. [21]

2. They "have greatly injured the cause of truth." [22]

3. They "make Christian duties . . . burdensome." [23]

4. They "raise a false standard and then endeavor to bring everybody [up] to it." [24]

5. Their spiritual eyesight is "perverted." [25]

6. Satan uses them "to cast contempt upon the work of the [Holy] Spirit." [26]

At the heart of the philosophy of ancient Greece was the idea of not-too-much, not-too-little: " 'Nothing to excess' *(Medan agan)* was their central doctrine, . . . which the Roman poet Horace later interpreted as 'the golden mean.' " [27]

Ellen White interpreted it in her own characteristically inimitable way: "True temperance teaches us to dispense entirely"—total abstinence—"with everything hurtful and to use judiciously that which is healthful." [28]

And to those who went to the ultimate extreme in "going overboard"—leaving the remnant church entirely—her warning to Dudley M. Canright (who did just that, in spite of her warnings) [29] remains as a timely caution today. Whether from skepticism and doubt, or from going to extreme positions, the tragedy is the same: making "shipwreck" of faith (1 Tim. 1:19). [30]

Conclusion

Ellen White began her ministry in 1844 by viewing in vision "a straight and narrow path, cast up high above the world." It was to become an ever-recurring theme; the expression "narrow path" alone would appear at least 135 times in her published writings during the next 70 years.

In 1879 she was concerned about "the dangers of youth," on a "downward road strewn with tempting pleasures which look very inviting" but at the end of which "death is there." She wrote earnestly to her church:

"The narrow path to life may appear to them to be destitute of attractions, a path of thorns and briers, but it is not. It is the path which requires a denial of sinful pleasures; it is a narrow path, cast up for the ransomed of the Lord to walk in. None can walk this path and carry with them their burdens of pride, self-will, deceit, falsehood, dishonesty, passion, and the carnal lusts. The path is so narrow that these things will have to be left behind by those who walk in it, but the broad road is wide enough for sinners to travel it with all their sinful propensities." [31]

Finally, 60 years after her first vision, as she was drawing toward the close of her ministry, she concluded the final chapter ("The Reward of Earnest Labor") of *Testimonies for the Church* with these three paragraphs of encouragement:

"We are homeward bound. He who loved us so much as to die for us hath builded for us a city. The New Jerusalem is our place of rest. There will be no sadness in the city of God. No wail of sorrow, no dirge of crushed hopes and buried affections, will evermore be heard. Soon the garments of heaviness will be changed for the wedding garment. Soon we shall witness the coronation of our King.

"Those whose lives have been hidden with Christ, those who on this earth have fought the good fight of faith, will shine forth with the Redeemer's glory in the kingdom of God.

"It will not be long till we shall see Him in whom our hopes of eternal life are centered. And in His presence, all the trials and sufferings of this life will be as nothingness. 'Cast not away therefore your confidence, which hath great recompense of reward. For ye have need of patience, that, after ye have done the will of God, ye might receive the promise. For yet a little while, and He that shall come will come, and will not tarry.' (Heb. 10:35-37). Look up, look up, and let your faith continually increase. *Let this faith guide you along the narrow path that leads through the gates of the city of God into the great beyond, the wide, unbounded future of glory that is for the redeemed.* 'Be patient therefore, brethren, unto the coming of the Lord. Behold, the husbandman waiteth for the precious fruit of the earth, and hath long patience for it, until he receive the early and latter rain. Be ye also patient; stablish your hearts: for the coming of the Lord draweth nigh' (James 5:7, 8)." [32]

Notes and References

[1] DA 149; cf. also Roger W. Coon, "The Bible, Ellen White, and Alcohol" (unpublished monograph, May 30, 1990).

[2] "Joseph Smith," *World Book Encyclopedia* (1990), vol. 17, pp. 517, 518.

[3] "Samuel S. Snow," SDAE 357.

[4] Arthur L. White in 1Bio 55 correctly identifies the landlord as Mrs. Elizabeth Haines; the address he gives for her home, however, is now known to be incorrect.

[5] EW 13.

[6] RPSDA 91, 73.

[7] *Ibid.,* p. 92.

[8] God's first choice was William Ellis Foy in 1842, and His second choice was Hazen Foss in 1844. (See separate biographical sketches in SDAE 473-475.)

[9] Roger W. Coon, *A Gift of Light* (Washington, D.C.: Review and Herald Pub. Assn., 1983), pp. 30, 31.

[10] EW 14, 15. Ellen's use of the descriptive adverb "rashly" in describing the denial of faith is both interesting and significant, for it prefigures a philosophy of faith that would slowly develop over the subsequent years, finding a more full characterization in the two metaphors "transaction" and "covenant" (DA 347). Ultimately Ellen would come to envisage faith as a seven-step process in which God took the first four steps before asking man to take the remaining three (see Roger W. Coon, "How Jesus Treated Thomas—The Pessimistic Doubter" [unpublished monograph, May 8, 1990], pp. 4-6).

[11] Rom. 13:13; 1 Cor. 7:17; Gal. 5:16, 25; Eph. 5:2, 8; Phil. 3:16; Col. 2:6; 4:5.

[12] 1 Cor. 9:24-26; Gal. 2:2; 5:7; Phil. 2:16; 2 Tim. 4:7; Heb. 12:1.

[13] UL 39.

[14] 2SM 477.

[15] 1T 425.

[16] CD 211.

[17] 3SM 217; the immediate context is a discussion of the proper age for a child's first entry into school.

[18] 4T 505.

[19] 5T 644; cf. TM 228; CH 628.

[20] Ev 611.

[21] 1T 212.

[22] 3T 315.

[23] 2SM 319.

[24] 2T 375.

[25] Ev 610, 611; cf. ST, Aug. 1, 1895.

[26] GC 10.

[27] "Ancient Greece: The Heritage of the Ancient Greeks," *Compton's Encyclopedia* (1982), vol. 10, p. 226.

[28] PP 562.

[29] 5T 571-573. The story is told—and illustrated—in Roger W. Coon, *"Look a Little Higher"* (Silver Spring, Md.: Ellen G. White Estate, Inc., 1990), pp. 10, 11.

[30] See 4T 233, 246; 5T 275, 675, 676.
[31] 4T 364.
[32] 9T 287, 288. (Italics supplied.)

CHAPTER 2

THE RANDOLPH VISION
"A Large Bible"

Winter 1845-1846

LET us direct our attention now to the winter of 1845-1846. Ellen Harmon had now been a prophetess for about one year, her first vision having come in December 1844, a short time after her seventeenth birthday. She had been slowly enlarging the sphere of her influence; invitations began to trickle in from companies of ex-Millerites, here and there, who were eager to see and hear firsthand the amazing experience of this young woman.

But travel in the mid-1840s was fraught with difficulties. Awed by the enormity of the undertaking, she wrote: "The work looked great, and the trials severe."

Three Kinds of Problems

1. *Physical problems:* "My health was very poor," [1] she later recorded in her first autobiographical account. She suffered from an advanced, debilitating form of tuberculosis, which also adversely affected her heart. At night she could generally breathe only when propped up in bed into a near sitting position. And she frequently was forced to spit up blood. [2] "My lungs and throat were very sore," she continued; consequently "it was with the greatest difficulty that I could speak aloud." Often she would begin her public presentations in a hoarse, raspy whisper, before the power of God would come upon her and give her miraculous (though often only temporary) healing. [3]

She ventured forth on her first speaking assignment in late January 1845. At five feet two inches in height and weighing but 80 pounds, [4] the near-invalid prophetess was obliged to crouch in the bottom of a sleigh, with a heavy buffalo robe thrown over her for protection from the merciless elements of a harsh New England winter. Her audience was a group of neighbors gathered at a married sister's home in Poland, Maine, some 30 miles from Portland. [5]

2. *Travel problems:* "The idea of a [single, teenage] female traveling [unchaperoned] from place to place caused me to draw back," she later admitted. [6]

Thus, on a trip to Orrington, Maine (where she would, for the first time, meet the man who in 1846 was to become her husband), she went in the company of a "Bro. J" and his sister. [7] On a trip to New Hampshire her travel companions were a sister-in-law, Louisa Foss; a "Bro. Files and his wife"; and future fiancé, James White. [8] On her first two trips south to Massachusetts Ellen was accompanied by her own sister, Sarah Harmon. [9]

(Of Ellen's seven brothers and sisters, only Sarah and Robert would follow her, along with their parents, in becoming Sabbath-keeping Adventists.)

But even with the precaution of impeccable chaperonage, Ellen did not escape the gossip of slanderous tongues. Almost immediately she received a distressing letter from her mother, begging her to return forthwith to her Portland home, because of "false reports," already in circulation, that sullied her reputation. "This," Ellen commented, with simple naïveté, "I had not expected." [10]

3. *Professional problems:* Among the most trying of her problems was the necessity of rebuking heretical teachings and fanatical practices, thereby suffering consequent personal attacks from extremist advocates.

Some continued to set successive dates for the Second Coming. The failure of Christ to appear at the times prescribed served only to compound disappointment, thus weakening further the faith of those who supported these false predictions. [11]

Others, taking a different tack, said that the Second Coming was in reality "spiritual," rather than a literal, personal appearing of our Saviour. [12]

Then there were those who "trusted every impression, and laid aside reason and judgment." [13] For many in this "rank fanaticism," this mindless blind following of "impressions and burdens . . . led to corruption, instead of [to] purity and holiness." [14] (The insidious and eventually adulterous practice of "spiritual wifery" was one such form of fanaticism!) [15]

She also had to meet those who "seemed to think that religion consisted in making a noise [literally, as well as figuratively!]. They would talk in such a manner as to irritate unbelievers, and cause them to hate them, and then they would rejoice that they suffered persecution." [16]

Frequently Ellen was called to deal with those practicing hypnotism. In those days this phenomenon often went under such quaint labels as "animal magnetism," [17] "spiritual magnetism," [18] or "mesmerism" [19] (after Franz—or Friedrich—Anton Mesmer, 1734-1815, an Austrian physician who popularized the practice). [20]

Some blatantly accused Ellen of originating her visions through self-hypnosis, [21] while others averred that her fiancé, James White, induced her trances by means of mesmerism. [22]

Joseph Turner, an ex-Millerite preacher who led an extreme splinter group in Maine, [23] boasted an expertise in mesmerism. He claimed not only that he could induce her hypnotically but also that he could prevent her from either having or telling a vision in his presence. Upon one occasion he himself attempted to put her into a trance by a bizarre performance:

"I arose in the congregation," Ellen wrote in her first autobiography. "My visions came up fresh before me, and I commenced relating them, when I felt a human influence being exerted against me. I looked at J. T. He had his hands up to his face, and was looking through his fingers, his eyes intently fixed upon me. His lips were compressed, and a groan now and then escaped him. In a moment I remembered the promise which the Lord had given me . . . that if I was in danger of being affected by a human influence, to ask for another angel, who would be sent to protect me. I then raised my hands to heaven, and earnestly cried, Another angel, Father! another angel! I knew that my request was granted. I felt shielded by the strong Spirit of the Lord, and was borne above every earthly influence, and with freedom finished my testimony." [24]

And, of course, spiritualism in its most unvarnished form had to be met, repeatedly. [25]

The strangest theological ideas were advocated by a lunatic fringe: some, for example, held that "there was no Holy Spirit, and that all the exercises that holy men of God [in Bible times] have experienced were only mesmerism or the deceptions of Satan." [26]

Others took extreme views of certain scriptural passages "and refrained wholly from labor, and rejected all those who would not receive their views on this point, and some other things which they held to be religious duties." [27]

A typical example was to be found in Paris, Maine, in an ex-Methodist preacher named Jesse Stevens. He was particularly influential because of his "zeal for the truth, and apparent holy living." A strong advocate of the "no-work" view, he (as did many of his fellow leaders) vehemently denounced those who disagreed with his views. Ellen was given a special testimony for Stevens, but "he rejected every evidence which the Lord gave to convince him of his error, and was firm to take nothing back in his course. He followed impressions and went [on] weary journeys, walking great distances, where he would only receive abuse, and considered that he was suffering for Christ's sake." [28]

Thus were the early energies of the new teenage prophetess expended, a particularly difficult and traumatic task because of her acute sensitivity to the feelings of others. As she herself shared:

"It was very crossing for me to relate to individuals what I had been shown concerning their wrongs. It caused me great distress to see others troubled or grieved. And when obligated to declare the messages, I often softened them down and related what I had seen as favorable for the individual as I could, and then would go by myself and weep in agony of spirit. . . . How could I relate the plain, cutting testimonies given me of God?" [29]

She summed up her mixed emotions, frustrations, and occasional feelings of despair in these words: "These were troublesome times. If we had not stood stiffly then, we should have made shipwreck of our faith. Some said we were stubborn; but we were obliged to set our faces as a flint, and turn not to the right hand nor to the left." [30]

Opposition of Sargent and Robbins

On Ellen and Sarah's second visit to Massachusetts they again stayed in the home of Otis Nichols, an Adventist lithographer of Dorchester (then nine miles from downtown Boston, today a part of south Boston). Ex-Millerites, Nichols and his wife were among the first to accept Bates's teaching on the seventh-day Sabbath; they began to observe it in 1845.

The Nicholses were happy to provide both hospitality and

transportation, for they ardently believed from the start that Ellen's visions were from the Lord; they also were a principal source of emotional support to the young prophetess. [31]

Just as Paul wrote gratefully of Onesiphorous, who "oft refreshed me, and was not ashamed of my chain" (2 Tim. 1:16), Ellen expressed heartfelt appreciation for this family who "were ever ready with words of encouragement to comfort me . . . and often their prayers ascended to heaven in my behalf." [32]

Nor were they ashamed of Ellen's "chain"—the "slings and arrows" of her "outraged" critics!

One morning after Ellen and Sarah had taken up residence, two self-styled leaders of an extremist group based in Boston (but with adherents as far afield as Randolph, 13 miles south) called at the Nichols' home to see Otis. The message of these fanatics may perhaps be best summed up as: (1) it is a sin to labor; (2) Christians should now sell all their property and give alms; (3) the church has now entered into the jubilee period, and even the land should rest; (4) the poor must be supported without labor on their part; (5) Ellen Harmon and her visions are directly of the devil. [33]

There appears to be some evidence that Sargent and Robbins once supported Ellen's prophetic gift, as had Joseph Turner; but all turned against her when her visions exposed the unbiblical nature of their respective teachings and practices. [34]

Upon this occasion Sargent and Robbins had come, ostensibly, to seek a favor of Nichols, and apparently to remain overnight. But when Otis informed them that Ellen Harmon was inside the house and invited them in to become acquainted with her, they suddenly remembered pressing business elsewhere. They said they must leave immediately. [35]

Before parting, however, Robbins solemnly declared that Ellen's visions were of the devil. How could he be so sure? Nichols inquired. Because, according to Robbins, he "always felt a blessing" whenever he declared they were of Satan! Nichols retorted that this kind of subjective test was unsafe. For himself, he accepted Ellen's gift as from the Lord on the basis of the objective evidence of the fruitage that they had already borne in those who had accepted them.

To preserve appearances, it was mutually decided that Ellen would come to Boston the very next Sabbath to present personally her views before the followers of Sargent and Robbins; then each could make his or her final determination as to the merits of her experience. [36]

But on the evening preceding the Sabbath Ellen was taken off in vision during family prayers. "I was shown," she later wrote, "that we must not go into Boston, but in an opposite direction to Randolph; that the Lord had a work for us to do there." [37]

Somewhat aggrieved, Nichols objected; he had given his word that he would produce Ellen at the meeting in Boston the next day. If they failed to appear as promised, her credibility—and his—would be seriously compromised. "I do not understand it," he fumed.

"The Lord showed me that we would understand it when we got there," a confident Ellen responded. Then she elaborated upon what the angel had revealed:

1. Sargent and Robbins were hypocrites; they had no intention whatever of being in Boston on the Sabbath in question, and there would be no meeting there for her to attend.

2. Instead, Sargent and Robbins would themselves go south to Randolph, to meet with a large company there, many of whom sympathized with these fanatical teachers in their opposition to Ellen Harmon's visions. (Boston was nine miles north of Dorchester, where Ellen was staying; Randolph was four miles south.)

3. Ellen and the Nicholses were to go to Randolph to confront and confound her critics at a meeting in the home of a Mr. Thayer.

4. While in their midst, God would give Ellen a message calculated to convince any honest and unprejudiced among them that her work was truly of God and not of Satan. [38]

Confrontation in Randolph

So the Nicholses took Ellen to the Thayer home, arriving sometime during the latter part of the morning. There they found a meeting already in progress, led by Sargent and Robbins. When the door was opened, and they saw Ellen walking into the parlor, their duplicity was exposed. But there was no way of escape for them!

They continued their presentation, but as Ellen later noted rather dryly, "they did not have much freedom."

At a noontime intermission one in attendance shared her personal opinion that "good matter would be brought out" when the meeting resumed in the early afternoon. "I believe it," Mrs. Nichols responded, without giving away what the angel had already revealed concerning that which was to follow. For his part, Robbins brashly told Sarah Harmon that her sister Ellen could have no vision while in his presence. [39]

The session resumed about 1:00 p.m. Sargent, Robbins, and French prayed, following a brief song service. Then "one of us," said Nichols, "prayed for the Lord to lead this meeting." Ellen then prayed, but was soon taken off in vision. Five specific points were revealed in her vision, which are of particular interest. Said Ellen:

"[1] I was again shown the errors of R. and S., and others united with them. [2] I saw that they could not prosper; that truth would triumph in the end, and error be brought down. [3] I was shown that they were not honest, and [4] then I was carried into the future and shown something of the course they would pursue, that they would continue to despise the teachings of the Lord, despise reproof, and that they would be left in total darkness, to resist God's Spirit until their folly should be made manifest to all. [5] A chain of truth was presented to me from the Scriptures, in contrast with their errors." [40]

In a trancelike vision state the prophet is totally unaware of his or her immediate physical surroundings, so for an account of what happened next we must turn to eyewitness Otis Nichols' handwritten report (the original of which is on file in the vault of the White Estate). While praying, Ellen was taken off in vision "with extraordinary manifestations, and [she] continued talking in vision with a shrill voice which could be distinctly understood by all present, until about sundown.

"Sargent, Robbins, and French were much exasperated as well as excited to hear Sister White talk in vision, which they declared was of the devil. They exhausted all their influence and bodily strength to destroy the effect of the vision. They would unite in singing very loud, and then alternately would talk and read from the Bible in a loud voice in order that Ellen might not be heard, until their strength was exhausted and their hands would shake, so they could not read from the Bible.

"But amidst all this confusion and noise Ellen's clear and shrill voice as she talked in vision was distinctly heard by all present. The opposition of these men continued as long as they could talk and sing, notwithstanding some of their own friends rebuked them and requested them to stop. 'But,' says Robbins, 'you are bound to an idol.

You are worshiping a golden calf.'

"Mr. Thayer, the owner of the house, was not fully satisfied that her vision was of the devil, as Robbins declared it to be. He wanted it tested in some way. He had heard that visions of satanic power were arrested by opening the Bible and laying it on the person in vision, and asked Sargent if he would test it in this way, which he declined to do.

"Then Thayer took a heavy, large quarto family Bible which was lying on the table and seldom used, opened it, and laid it upon the breast of Ellen while in vision, as she was then inclined backward against the wall in one corner of the room.

"Immediately after the Bible was laid upon her, she arose upon her feet and walked into the middle of the room, with the Bible open in one hand and lifted as high as she could reach, and with her eyes steadily looking upward, declared in a solemn manner: 'The inspired testimony of God,' or words of the same import, and then she continued for a long time while the Bible was extended in one hand and her eyes looking upward and not on the Bible, to turn the leaves with the other hand and place her finger upon certain passages and correctly utter their words with a solemn voice.

"Many present [climbed up on chairs and] looked at the passages where her finger was pointed to see if she spoke them correctly, for her eyes at the same time were looking upward [at an angle so acute that she herself could not read these words].

"Some of the passages referred to were judgments against the wicked and blasphemous; and others were admonitions and instructions relative to our present condition.

"In this state she continued all the afternoon until nearly sundown when she came out of vision. When Ellen rose in vision upon her feet with the heavy open Bible upon her hand, and walked the room uttering the passages of Scripture, Sargent, Robbins, and French were silent. For the remainder of the time they were troubled, with many others, but they shut their eyes and braved it out without making any acknowledgment of their feelings." [41]

Interestingly, Ellen's specific predictions concerning the future situation of these critics were fulfilled in a rather dramatic manner. In a certain public meeting, according to Nichols' personal testimony, "Satan took control of their minds and led them to confess publicly some of the most shameful acts of their lives, which had the effect to break up the meetings at Randolph and separate the honest souls from their unholy influence."

Nichols added that about a year later, "They made a wreck of all their faith in the doctrines taught in the Bible and then broke up and scattered, declaring themselves free from all sinning. . . . Thus the curse of God was literally fulfilled upon those who obstinately continued to denounce the visions of Sister White after they had once been enlightened by them." [42]

An Authentic Miracle

Ellen had been in vision from about 1:00 p.m. until sunset; when she regained consciousness she noticed that "candles were burning. I had been in vision nearly four hours." [43] Note that during this time she did not breathe, and during much of it she held a large, heavy Bible in her unsupported outstretched hand. These were genuine miracles of God.

The Randolph vision is believed by specialists at the White Estate to have been her longest—"nearly four hours," according to her own estimate. By contrast, her shortest was probably a 30-second "flash-light" picture, given while she was praying during family worship one morning, according to her son, W. C. White, who was himself present. [44] James White, her husband of 35 years (who probably viewed his wife in the vision state more than any other individual), estimated that her visions typically ranged from 15 minutes to three hours. [45]

The four-hour vision at Randolph was not, however, the longest on record in the 1840s. William Ellis Foy, God's first choice for the prophetic office, received two visions in Boston in 1842. The first, on January 18, lasted two and a half hours; but the second, on February 4, ran a remarkable 12½ hours. [46]

In the vision state the prophet's heart continues to function normally, but the lungs are totally at rest—in vision the prophet simply does not breathe. There is usually a loss of normal strength, and often an infusion of supernatural strength. The eyes may be open, but the immediate surroundings are lost to view—rather, the prophet sees what God wishes him to see (whether of past, present, or future).

Probably the best biblical description of the physical condition of a prophet in vision is that found in the tenth chapter of the book of Daniel.

In Joel 2:28-32 we are informed that prophets also receive messages in the night season by means of prophetic dreams. The content of such dreams doubtless is indistinguishable from that received in daytime visions, the only apparent difference probably being the absence of physical phenomena at night.

Why Physical Phenomena?

Why, then, doesn't God give *all* His messages at night in prophetic dreams, in the privacy of the prophet's bedchamber? Why does He sometimes give His messages in daylight hours? Ellen White occasionally received visions before an audience of many, in an "open vision of the day," with dramatic, spectacular physical phenomena.

Arthur L. White, secretary of the White Estate for nearly half a century (1938-1978) and grandson of the prophetess, pondered this anomaly. He suggests why physical phenomena predominate in the *early* experience of a prophet:

"Such phenomenal exhibitions in connection with the early visions had a definite place in establishing the confidence of the believers in their divine origin before there was opportunity for the development of fruit by which the claims of the Lord's messenger might be judged." [47]

This correlates with Joel 2:28-32, where we read of young men seeing visions and old men dreaming prophetic dreams. Whether by coincidence or not, this was the way it was in Ellen White's own experience: in her earlier years the messages came by daytime visions; in the later years they came through prophetic dreams at night.

During the early years the church members, unacquainted with her experience, needed an abundance of immediate, visual (and often visceral!) evidence to alert them to the fact that God was here at work. In her earliest writings one finds frequent reference to "I was shown," "the angel said," etc. In the later years, when her prophethood was largely established within the church, the public visions—and the direct references to the supernatural source of their content—became less and less a part of her ministry.

Physical phenomena certainly is impressive. For many in Ellen

White's day it put the capsheaf to individual conviction that her message was truly from God. Daniel T. Bourdeau's experience is a case in point.

Bourdeau, at 22, was a new believer in the Advent message but *not* a believer in its prophetess. On June 21, 1857, however, he witnessed Ellen White in vision, and became a true believer! Of this experience he wrote:

"I was an unbeliever in the visions; but one circumstance among others that I might mention convinced me that her visions were of God.

"To satisfy my mind as to whether she breathed or not, I first put my hand on her chest sufficiently long to know that there was no more heaving of the lungs than there would have been had she been a corpse. I then took my hand and placed it over her mouth, pinching her nostrils between my thumb and forefinger, so that it was impossible for her to exhale or inhale air, even if she had desired to do so. I held her thus with my hand about ten minutes, long enough for her to suffocate under ordinary circumstances; she was not in the least affected by this ordeal.

"Since witnessing this wonderful phenomenon, I have not once been inclined to doubt the divine origin of her visions." [48]

But a word of caution is necessary here. Satan, too, is a supernatural being—"the prince of the power of the air" (Eph. 2:2). Satan can—and does—counterfeit all of the physical phenomena associated with a prophet in a vision! This is why the Seventh-day Adventist Church, from earliest times, has taken the position that physical phenomena are a legitimate *evidence* that something supernatural is going on, but they are not *proof* that what is happening is emanating from the Lord!

Physical phenomena do not authenticate the validity of a prophet. Other biblically based tests can and must be applied, according to Mrs. White herself. [49]

But two things are certain: (a) Ellen White did *not* breathe for four hours one Sabbath afternoon in Randolph, Massachusetts, in the winter of 1845-1846, and (b) she *did* hold a large, heavy Bible in an unsupported outstretched hand during that vision for a considerable length of time. Nor was this the only time she held a large Bible in vision: at least three other instances appear to be historically documented during which this miracle took place, [50] between the winter of 1844-1845 and August 1848.

Some have been troubled that Arthur G. Daniells should have appeared to express doubt about such Bible-holding incidents in 1919. Daniells served the General Conference for the longest period as president (1901-1922); he was an original trustee and the first chairman of the board of the White Estate, and worked closely with Mrs. White from 1878 until her death in 1915. He wrote:

"I do not know whether that [holding a heavy Bible on out-stretched arm] was ever done or not. I am not sure. I did not see it, and I do not know that I ever talked with anybody that did see it. . . . Just how much of that is genuine, and how much has crawled into the story? I do not know." [51]

But the last of the four documented Bible-holding incidents took place in 1848, exactly 10 years before Daniells was born. So it is quite understandable why he never witnessed it himself!

But that is not the point: if you read the internal context of Daniells' entire statement, you quickly discover that his remarks were obviously intended to downplay the use of such miracle stories as *proof* of a prophet's authenticity or legitimacy. Evidence that something supernatural is happening? Yes! But proof of authenticity? No! Other tests must be applied. Basically, Daniells was protesting the wrong use of such miracle stories.

Conclusion

The ultimate evidence that Ellen White was a true prophet, for the people in Randolph, Massachusetts, on that mind-boggling day in the winter of 1845-1846 was not the miracle of her not breathing for four hours, nor that of holding a large Bible on an outstretched, unsupported hand. It was, rather, to be found in the content of the vision. 1. The unbiblical teachings of Sargent, Robbins, and company were exposed for what they were—theological fraud—by the Scriptures given to Ellen by God, which she uttered and pointed to during the vision. 2. She made a direct prediction concerning the future activities of her critics, which proved to be 100 percent correct within the space of several months.

Ellen White was a true prophet; and, with Peter, we may also say that "we have not followed cunningly devised fables" when we believed on this prophetess of modern times. On the contrary, "we have a more sure word of prophecy; whereunto ye do well that ye take heed, as unto a light that shineth in a dark place, until the day dawn, and the day star arise in your hearts" (2 Peter 1:16, 19).

Notes and References

[1] 2SG 36.

[2] RPSDA 92.

[3] 2SG 38.

[4] James White, *Life Incidents in Connection With the Great Advent Movement* (Battle Creek, Mich.: Steam Press of the Seventh-day Adventist Pub. Assn., 1868), p. 273.

[5] Bio 65.

[6] 2SG 36.

[7] *Ibid.,* p. 38.

[8] *Ibid.,* p. 46.

[9] *Ibid.,* pp. 71, 75.

[10] *Ibid.,* p. 39.

[11] *Ibid.,* p. 58.

[12] *Ibid.,* pp. 72, 74.

[13] *Ibid.,* p. 45.

[14] *Ibid.,* p. 50.

[15] *Ibid.,* pp. 68, 42; cf. 1Bio 82, 223; 8MR 226; DF 733.

[16] 2SG 50, 51.

[17] 2SM 352.

[18] 2SG 46.

[19] *Ibid.,* p. 48.

[20] *Webster's Biographical Dictionary* (Springfield, Mass.: G. & C. Merriam Co., 1974), p. 1012.

[21] 2SG 57.

[22] Transcript, statement of Otis Nichols, unpublished document, DF 105, pp. 3, 4. The document is handwritten and signed but undated. It is believed to have been written in 1859 or 1860 (1Bio 103), since Ellen White quotes three paragraphs of it in 2SG 77-79 (published in 1860).

[23] "Joseph Turner," SDAE 1507, 1508.

[24] 2SG 62, 63.

[25] *Ibid.,* pp. 72, 74.

[26] *Ibid.,* p. 58.

[27] *Ibid.*

[28] *Ibid.,* pp. 63, 64.

[29] *Ibid.,* p. 60.

[30] *Ibid.,* p. 74.

[31] "Otis Nichols," SDAE 975. Printer Nichols is also remembered for preparing prophetic charts used by early Seventh-day Adventist evangelists.

[32] 2SG 68.

[33] *Ibid.,* p. 75.

[34] Nichols, pp. 4, 5.

[35] 2SG 75.

[36] Nichols, p. 4.

[37] 2SG 76.

[38] Cited in RPSDA 117, 118.

[39] 2SG 76.

[40] *Ibid.,* pp. 76, 77; cf. Nichols, p. 4.

[41] Nichols, pp. 5-7.

[42] *Ibid.,* pp. 7, 8.

[43] 2SG 79, 77.

[44] Cited in Arthur L. White, *Ellen G. White: Messenger to the Remnant* (Washington, D.C.: Review and Herald Pub. Assn., 1969), p. 8.

[45] James White, p. 272.

[46] Delbert W. Baker, *The Unknown Prophet* (Hagerstown, Md.: Review and Herald Pub. Assn., 1987), pp. 21, 88, 105, 106.

[47] Arthur L. White, *Messenger to the Remnant,* p. 26.

[48] Cited in RPSDA 97. Arthur White corrects Bourdeau's inadvertent misstatement of date in 1Bio 357.

[49] See Roger W. Coon, *Heralds of New Light: Another Prophet to the Remnant?* (Boise, Idaho: Pacific Press Pub. Assn., 1987), pp. 13-21.

[50] Incident 1: Winter 1844-1845, Portland, Maine, Ellen G. White's third vision, cited in GSAM 236, 237. Incident 2: Winter 1844-1845, Topsham, Maine, cited in GSAM 237, 238. Incident 3: Randolph vision, cited above. Incident 4: August 1848, Hannibal, New York, cited in LS 110-112. Cf. Ron Graybill, "Ellen G. White and the Big Bible," *Insight,* Feb. 2, 1985, pp. 8-10.

[51] Cited in *Spectrum* 10 No. 1 (May 1979): 28.

THE HEAVENLY SANCTUARY VISION
"The Reality"

April 3, 1847

LLEN Harmon had been a unique prophetic "messenger" of the Lord for nearly one year and nine months when she exchanged her family name for that of her fiancé, James White, on August 30, 1846. Poor as the proverbial church mice, the newlyweds initially made their new home with Ellen's parents in Gorham, Maine, where she had been born some 19 years earlier (Gorham is located about 12 miles west of Portland). [1]

Robert Harmon, Sr., and his wife, Eunice, believed in the divine origin of their daughter's visions, but they were not as quick to accept her new ideas concerning the obligation of New Testament Christians to observe the Sabbath on Saturday (and would not for at least another year). [2] Thus normal in-law tensions in the home were exacerbated by religious differences; it was inevitable that the new couple would need to find other living quarters elsewhere within a half year.

But this was perhaps among the least of their immediate problems. Within several months of their wedding, Satan appears to have made two concerted efforts to snuff out the life of the young prophetess—though not without advance warning from the Lord. Wrote Ellen: "I was shown that I would be much afflicted, and that we would have a trial of our faith after our return to Gorham." [3]

First came a life-threatening illness in November 1846. Never in robust health since the age of 9 (she was suffering from advanced tuberculosis and lung hemorrhages at the time of her call to the prophetic office at age 17), the young bride was now felled by an affliction that prostrated her. Indeed, after three weeks her condition was so traumatic that she requested no further prayers be offered on her behalf, preferring death to continued suffering.

At a special prayer season for her recovery, Henry Nichols, son of the Adventist lithographer of Dorchester, Massachusetts (an earlier benefactor), felt led of the Spirit to pray for her restoration. Ellen wrote later:

"Much burdened, and with the power of God resting upon him, [Henry] rose from his knees, came across the room, and laid his hands upon my head, saying, 'Sister Ellen, Jesus Christ maketh thee whole,' and fell back prostrated by the power of God. I believed the work was of God, and the pain left me. My soul was filled with gratitude and peace." [4]

But Satan was not finished with her. Several weeks later Ellen and her husband traveled from Portland to Boston by ship. During the voyage a severe storm blew up suddenly, though not unexpectedly, for the North Atlantic is well known to punish travelers who dare to venture out upon her waters in winter months.

The passengers were terrified, most despairing of their lives, for the vessel itself was severely damaged. Struck by the contrast of Ellen's calm demeanor and self-possession, a fellow traveler queried her, whereupon the latter responded:

"I told her I made Christ my refuge, and if my work was done, I might as well lie in the bottom of the ocean as in any other place; but if my work was not done, all the waters of the ocean could not drown me. My trust was in God, that He would bring us safe to land if it was for His glory." [5]

It was, and He did! But one of Satan's titles in Scripture is "prince of the power of the air"; and it is quite likely that Satan was hoping—either through acute illness or a severe storm at sea—to destroy God's chosen instrument, thus to put a premature end to her work before she could do him much damage. Nor would this be the last time that he would attempt such a feat!

In the autumn of 1846 James and Ellen had occasion to read a tract written by retired sea captain-turned-Millerite preacher, Joseph Bates, in which the author strenuously held for the present sanctity and Christian obligation of the seventh-day Sabbath. Though only 48 pages in length, the tract bore the rather ponderous title of *The Seventh-day Sabbath, a Perpetual Sign, From the Beginning, to the*

Entering Into the Gates of the Holy City, According to the Commandment!

The Scriptures adduced were impressive and the logic coercive, whereupon the Whites, out of a simple commitment to basic Christian honesty, accepted this new doctrine. They began to observe, teach, and defend it before others. At this time there were perhaps 50 Sabbathkeepers in all of New England and New York State among the ranks of the disappointed ex-Millerites. [6]

A Significant Vision

In early 1847 the Whites accepted an invitation from the Stockbridge Howland family to come and live on the top floor of their spacious, well-constructed home. Topsham was some 35 miles north of their former residence at Gorham. It was here, on Sabbath, April 3, before a small group of assembled fellow Sabbathkeepers, that 19-year-old Ellen was given one of her most important visions.

This vision is recognized as significant by the church today for at least three reasons: 1. It repeated, and enlarged upon, the content of a vision given four weeks earlier, on March 6, in which the existence and reality of the heavenly sanctuary inside the New Jerusalem were revealed in major, substantive detail for the first time. [7]

2. These two visions confirmed James and Ellen's prior Bible study that the Saturday Sabbath was still binding upon New Testament Christians. They came six to seven months after the Whites had accepted and begun to observe this day. (The Whites did not keep the Sabbath because the visions told them to do so; the visions came after Bible study, serving only to confirm it—Seventh-day Adventists did not get their doctrines from the visions, but rather from hard, diligent Bible study and earnest prayer!)

3. Ellen's theological understanding was enlarged by these two visions when, for apparently the first time, she grasped the truth that the Sabbath has eschatological implications and significance. Now she tied it to the end-time "mark" of the "beast" of the third angel's message of Revelation 14:9-11. (Joseph Bates had made the linkage a little earlier, and incorporated it into the second edition of *Perpetual Sign,* published in August 1846. [8]

A Real Sanctuary

Four days after this impressive vision, Ellen wrote of it in detail to

Joseph Bates. Please note in particular the prepositions she employed in describing this mind-boggling cosmic journey to the celestial city:

"Soon I was lost to earthly things and was wrapped in a vision of God's glory. I saw an angel flying swiftly to me. He quickly carried me from the earth *to* the Holy City. *In* the city I saw a temple, which I entered. I passed *through* a door before I came *to* the first veil. This veil was raised, and I passed *into* the holy place. Here I saw the altar of incense, the candlestick with seven lamps, and the table on which was the shewbread. After viewing the glory of the holy, Jesus raised the second veil and I passed *into* the holy of holies.

"*In* the holiest I saw an ark; on the top and sides of it was purest gold. On each end of the ark was a lovely cherub, with its wings spread out *over* it. Their faces were turned toward each other, and they looked downward. *Between* the angels was a golden censer. *Above* the ark, where the angels stood, was an exceeding bright glory, that appeared like a throne where God dwelt. Jesus stood *by* the ark, and as the saints' prayers came up to Him, the incense in the censer would smoke, and He would offer up their prayers with the smoke of the incense to His Father.

"*In* the ark was the golden pot of manna, Aaron's rod that budded, and the tables of stone which folded together like a book. Jesus opened them, and I saw the Ten Commandments written *on* them with the finger of God. *On* one table were four, and *on* the other six. The four *on* the first table shone brighter than the other six. But the fourth, the Sabbath commandment, shone above them all; for the Sabbath was set apart to be kept in honor of God's holy name. The holy Sabbath looked glorious—a halo of glory was all *around* it." [9]

This vision was indeed impressive, and Ellen was totally struck with the reality of the experience: she was in a real place, accompanied by real supernatural personages, and looking at real liturgical furniture, concerning which she previously had only read about in Scripture. Forever after she would represent this heavenly temple— and its High Priest—as something very real, very literal.

As Seventh-day Adventists began to develop their theological bearings during the next three years and formulate their belief structure, this "sanctuary doctrine" would become paramount in their thinking.

While all of the doctrines of the Bible are true, and certainly important (God wouldn't have put them there if they weren't!), yet all doctrines are not of equal stature and standing. Ellen quickly came to differentiate among them by means of an interesting metaphor, the chief elements of which are: (a) a "solid, immovable platform," (b) four principal "pillars" that support the platform, and (c) "three steps" that serve the dual functions of supporting the platform (as do the "pillars") and providing entry to it. [10]

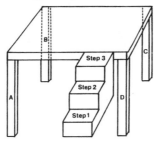

Interpreting her own symbols, Ellen explained that the "platform" of "truth"—not merely truth as propositional "theory," nor yet truth as "controversial subject," but rather the truth "as it is in Jesus" [11]—was the total doctrinal construct of the newly developing church.

The pillar doctrines were chiefly those that support the four corners of that platform—cardinal teachings such as the second coming of Christ, conditional immortality ("soul sleep"), the seventh-day Sabbath (in the greater framework of the immutable Law of God), and the high priesthood of Jesus Christ in His heavenly sanctuary. [12]

And the "three steps"? The three angels' messages of Revelation 14 not only support the total framework of "present truth," but also provide the key to unlock contemporary meaning and open the door of understanding. [13]

Early Opposition

Of all the pillar doctrines, the doctrine of Christ's high priesthood in the sanctuary above was "especially" validated by the Holy Spirit "over and over again" and "in a marked manner," more than any of the others. [14] Also, it alone constitutes the unique contribution of Seventh-day Adventists to the theology of Protestant Christendom, "the very message that has made us a separate people, and has given character and power to our work." [15]

This doctrine, of all those held by Seventh-day Adventists, was probably the first to be attacked, initially within the church and later from without.

In the mid-1860s, B. F. Snook and W. H. Brinkerhoff, officers in the Iowa Conference, broke away to form the "Marion Party," one of the first offshoot movements Adventism would experience. There is some evidence that opposition to the sanctuary doctrine was among their heretical tenets. [16]

Some 30 years later Dudley M. Canright, one of Adventism's most effective public evangelists, left the faith to fight it. In his *Seventh-day Adventism Renounced,* published in 1889, two years after his defection, Canright devoted an entire chapter to attacking our position on the sanctuary. [17]

Just after the turn of the century Albion Fox Ballenger and Dr. John Harvey Kellogg joined the anti-sanctuary ranks. Both attacked not only the doctrine itself, but also its chief "messenger."

Ballenger, an Adventist minister who subsequently apostatized to form an offshoot movement, made a frontal attack against the idea that Jesus had a two-apartment post-Calvary ministry in the heavenly sanctuary. His influence was substantial, and Ellen White summoned him to the new Washington, D.C., headquarters of the General Conference for a face-to-face confrontation. [18]

Dr. Kellogg's opposition was more indirect and insidious—and therefore the more dangerous. Kellogg, medical superintendent who made the Battle Creek Sanitarium world-famous, was undoubtedly the best-known Seventh-day Adventist around the world in 1903. He was also a most powerful person within the church, second only to Ellen White herself. [19]

His pet intellectual diversion was pantheism, which he couched in his cleverly crafted book *The Living Temple.* Ellen White declared that this volume (1) contained the "alpha" of "deadly heresies"; (2) that the "omega" would as surely follow it, being of "a most startling nature"; and (3) she trembled for the Adventist people. [20]

The good doctor did not address the issue of a heavenly sanctuary per se in his work, but the implications of his heresy were enormous. W. A. Spicer, newly elected secretary of the General Conference (April 11, 1903), sat down with Kellogg to discuss the book and its implications.

"Where is heaven?" Spicer asked Kellogg. The doctor then urged him to understand that "heaven is where God is, and God is everywhere—in the grass, in the trees, in all creation."

"To explain the sanctuary that Scripture declares is to be cleansed," the doctor pointed to his heart: "The sin is here, and here is the sanctuary to be cleansed." [21]

In another vision of the great "platform" of the truth "as it is in Jesus," Ellen White saw "one high in responsibility in the medical work" [Kellogg] rummaging around down underneath it, examining the various pillars and ordering his associates to "loosen the timbers supporting this platform."

Then she heard a voice from heaven rhetorically inquiring if the church were prepared to "permit this man to present doctrines that deny the past experience of the people of God."

Addressing Dr. Kellogg's professional medical colleagues, many of whom had adopted his pantheistic views, Mrs. White pointed out the sure result were the church to espouse such views:

"The principles of truth that God in His wisdom has given to the remnant church would be discarded. Our religion would be changed. The fundamental principles which have supported the work for the past fifty years would be accounted as error. A new organization would be established. Books of a new order would be written. A system of intellectual philosophy would be introduced." [22]

In spite of Ellen White's clear-cut declarations concerning the heavenly sanctuary and the high-priesthood ministry of Jesus in it, "no sanctuary" views continued to raise their ugly heads past the time of her death. In the 1930s William Warde Fletcher in Australia and L. R. Conradi in Europe continued to espouse such views. In the 1980s Desmond Ford was their most eloquent and articulate spokesman.

The basic thesis of the critics generally revolves around the idea that there really is no objective sanctuary in heaven, that Ellen White's 1847 visions were merely an allegorical parable in which the great truth of Christ's atonement was illustrated, perhaps something like the experience of Daniel where he sees four terrifying "beasts" appearing to rise from the sea—to teach a lesson. But those beasts weren't "real" (though they probably must have seemed so to Daniel, who may even have taken a step backward during the vision to distance himself from them!).

Allegory Versus Reality

Did Ellen White ever have "parable-like" visions? Indeed she did; the one in which she saw her husband in his bedroom, and Dr. Kellogg in his bedroom, each crouching over a strange pile of boulders, preparing to "stone" each other, is a good example. [23]

Was the 1847 vision also of a "parable" nature, or is there a literal sanctuary/temple in heaven that Ellen White visited in company with an angel and Jesus Himself? Let the woman speak for herself. In chapter 23 ("What Is the Sanctuary?") in *The Great Controversy* Mrs. White spoke of the work of early Seventh-day Adventist pioneers in these cogent, trenchant words:

"Those who were studying the subject found *indisputable proof* of the existence of a sanctuary in heaven. Moses made the earthly sanctuary after a pattern which was shown him. Paul teaches that the pattern was the true sanctuary which is in heaven. And John testifies that he saw it in heaven." [24]

Indeed, in 1864, in some of her earliest writing on the sanctuary, Ellen White had declared that Christ on Sinai "presented before Moses a miniature model of the heavenly sanctuary." [25]

SDA Theological Seminary professor C. Mervyn Maxwell has helpfully pointed out that in the Greek Septuagint translation of the Bible the terms *paradeigma* of Exodus 25:9 and *tupon* (from *tupis)* of Hebrews 8:5 may both properly be translated as "model." [26]

Ellen White believed in a real, literal sanctuary in heaven!

Mrs. White was greatly concerned about those who would "spiritualize away" the great truths of God's Word. [27] She knew allegory when she saw it, saw a genuine (if limited) value in it, and publicly expressed appreciation for John Bunyan's *Pilgrim's Progress.* [28] But she also knew her Christian church history; and she doubtless remembered the excesses of certain learned Christian theologians (especially Clement of Alexandria and Origen [second and third centuries A.D.]) who "would see an allegorical meaning in almost every passage of the Bible and sometimes deny a literal sense altogether." [29]

And she was aware of the potential for theological damage in misusing allegory in the twentieth century as well. A classic example we may cite is the doctrine that teaches that the personage identified by the name Satan in Scripture is not a real supernatural being but merely a metaphorical figure of speech to personify evil.[30] Mrs. White taught that this would be an especially pernicious teaching "as we approach the close of time" in the "last campaign." [31]

A similar heresy of an allegorical nature—"the doctrine that there is no sanctuary"—not only was clearly identified as one of a number of dangerous "false theories," but the prediction was made categorically that "in the future" "this is one of the points on which there will be a departing from the faith." [32]

Conclusion

(1) Ellen White's interesting employment of certain prepositions in her description of the 1847 visions, (2) her flat declaration that Moses, Paul, and John in Scripture give us "indisputable proof " of the existence of a real heavenly sanctuary, (3) her designation of the "no sanctuary" theory as heretical in her day, and (4) her forecast that in the time following her death this false theory would again arise leave us in no doubt as to where she stood on this issue.

But the existence of a real sanctuary or temple in heaven was not the only reason we remember the visions of March 6 and April 3, 1847. As mentioned above, this was the first confirmation *in vision* that Ellen White received that she and her husband were correct in keeping the seventh-day Sabbath.

Note also that the Holy Spirit came to Ellen White in vision after Bible study, to confirm positions already taken (or, on occasion, to correct false conclusions, or to suggest new directions if those studying the Word had come up against a brick wall and could go no further) rather than to initiate such positions. This was a foretaste of how the Spirit would operate in the next three years during the early Sabbath Conferences of 1848-1850, when our doctrinal framework was hammered out in thorough, exhaustive Bible study and prayer.[33]

Seventh-day Adventists received their doctrine of Sabbath sacredness from Bible study and prayer, not from the visions of Ellen White. The same may truthfully be said of every other doctrine that they teach—whether "pillar" or "platform."

Finally, in the last half of her written account of this interesting vision concerning the heavenly sanctuary, Ellen White probably for the first time linked the observance of the Sabbath with eschatological significance, tying it to the end-time "mark" of the "beast" of Revelation 14:9-11.[34]

Notes and References

[1] 1Bio 17, 113.

[2] *Ibid.,* p. 119.

[3] LS (1880) p. 239; cited in 1Bio 115.

[4] *Ibid.,* pp. 239, 240.

[5] *Ibid.,* p. 240.

[6] 1T 77.

[7] Paul A. Gordon has pointed out that Ellen White initially became aware of the existence of the heavenly sanctuary as a result of three visions (Feb. 1845; Oct. 1845, and sometime between Feb. and Apr. 1846) before the major revelations of March 6 at Fairhaven, Mass., and April 3, 1847, at Topsham, Maine, in which she herself personally visited the temple in heaven and was conducted into the Most Holy Place, among others. Historians are divided upon the *year* in which the Fairhaven vision took place (Mrs. White herself does not date it): Gordon (in *The Sanctuary, 1844, and the Pioneers* [Review and Herald, 1983], pp. 27, 28) and some other scholars tend to date it in March of 1846, because Mrs. White's reference (LS, pp. 95, 96) to it precedes, chronologically, her autobiographical account of her marriage to James White in Aug. 1846. Denominational historian C. Mervyn Maxwell (and some other scholars), however, identify the year as 1847, on the basis of Joseph Bates's declaration (when he published his "broadside" reporting the April 3, 1847 vision at Topsham) in Bates's personal postscript to his document—also dated April 3, 1847—where he added: "At a meeting in Fairhaven, 6th of last month, I saw her have a similar vision, which I then wrote down." Whether the Fairhaven vision of March 6 is to be dated in 1846 or 1847, however, it was this one—together with the Topsham vision of April 3, 1847—which conclusively proved to Ellen White that the sanctuary in heaven is a real, literal place. (Interview with C. Mervyn Maxwell, Jan. 24, 1991.)

[8] See C. Mervyn Maxwell, "Joseph Bates and Seventh-day Adventist Theology," Appendix G in Kenneth A. Strand, ed., *The Sabbath in Scripture and History* (Washington, D.C.: Review and Herald Pub. Assn., 1982), p. 356.

[9] EW 32, 33. (Italics supplied.)

[10] *Ibid.,* pp. 258, 259.

[11] RH, June 3, 1890.

[12] CW 30; the doctrine of the Second Advent is included by implication from the context.

[13] EW 258.

[14] Ev 224 (Ms 125, 1907).

[15] CW 54, *Special Testimonies,* Series B, No. 7 [1905] (p. 17).

[16] "Marion Party," SDAE 853, 854. Although documentary proof linking Snook and Brinkerhoff to an anti-sanctuary stand is today difficult to demonstrate, it must be remembered that these two were among the earliest founders of the Seventh Day Church of God, which today emphatically rejects the SDA sanctuary doctrine.

[17] Dudley M. Canright, *Seventh-Day Adventism Renounced* (Chicago: Fleming H. Revell Co., 1889), pp. 117-128; see also "Dudley Marvin Canright," SDAE 230, 231.

[18] "Albion Fox Ballenger," SDAE 121; 5Bio 404-413.

[19] "John Harvey Kellogg," SDAE 722, 723.

[20] 1SM 200, 197, 203; in a letter to her son Edson on March 15, 1905, Ellen further characterized Kellogg's pantheistic ideas as "false theories," "evil, seductive theories" "a dish of scientific fables" (UL 88).

[21] DF 15c, W. A. Spicer, "How the Spirit of Prophecy Met a Crisis," pp. 19, 20; cf. also p. 53.

[22] 1SM 204, 205.

[23] 3Bio 161, 162 (Ms. 2, 1880).

[24] GC 415. (Italics supplied.)

[25] 4aSG 5.

[26] Maxwell interview, Jan. 24, 1991.

[27] GC 674, 675.

[28] GC 252; MLT 73; COL 236, 253; 9T 217.

[29] "Allegory," *The Oxford Dictionary of the Christian Church* (1958), pp. 36, 37.

[30] GC 524; 1T 295.

[31] GC 516; 1T 341.

[32] CW 53 (RH, May 25, 1905); see also Ev 360 (Ms 11, 1906); 224 (Ms 125, 1907).

[33] " 'Sabbath Conferences,' " SDAE 1255, 1256; see also Roger W. Coon, "Ellen G. White's Role in the Development of SDA Doctrines" (unpublished lecture outline, Andrews University/SDA Theological Seminary, Jan. 30, 1992).

[34] EW 34; cf. 1Bio 121.

CHAPTER 4

THE "RAPPINGS" AND
"TRAIN OF CARS" VISIONS
"The Menace"

March 24, 1849 / August 24, 1850

AT the mention of the word "prophet," what is the immediate, almost instinctive, word association that is conjured in minds of most people? Doubtless, it is fortuneteller, predictor of the future, something of that sort. Probably coming in a close second and third in our sweepstakes race would be "miracle worker" and "a writer of the Bible."

It is interesting, then, that Jesus called His cousin John the Baptist the greatest of the prophets and "more than a prophet" (Matt. 11:11, 9). John's message was present tense, not future tense: "The Messiah is here!" We find no predictions of the future recorded over John's signature in Scripture. John Zebedee adds concerning his "Baptist" namesake, "John did no miracle" (John 10:41). And John the Baptist wrote not one verse of the New Testament.

Yet Jesus said he was the greatest prophet, indeed, even "more than a prophet." Obviously Jesus viewed the role of prophet much more differently than most Bible-believing Christians, then or now.

John the Baptist was, principally, a public proclaimer. No predictions of the future are attributable to him. Moses was chiefly an administrator, a lawgiver, a leader. Prediction forms an almost insignificant part of his Pentateuch (really, there are only a couple Messianic prophecies attributed to him). The apostle Paul was a theologian and a missionary. He wrote more than half the New Testament, but few miracles are credited to his name. And not very much is found in his writings with regard to predictions of the future.

What about Ellen White? She did pray with some people who were seriously ill, and they did recover their health; but very little in

49

the generally accepted sense of "miracle" is credited to her. Informed Adventists accept her writings as divinely inspired—in the
same manner, and to the same degree, as the writers of the Bible. Yet
the church steadfastly refuses to consider them a part of the sacred
canon of Scripture or a substitute for the Bible.

As for Ellen White making predictions, Robert W. Olson, who
retired in 1990 as executive secretary of the Ellen G. White Estate,
has offered his considered opinion that the predictive element really
does not loom large in the total bulk of Mrs. White's writings.
Perhaps a mere 5 percent of the total 25 million words she is
believed to have penned during the 70 years of her ministry
(1844-1915) could be classed as predictive.

Mrs. White confounded her friends and elated her enemies when,
in two services in the Battle Creek Tabernacle, on October 1 and 2,
1904, she said simply, "I do not claim to be a prophetess." [1]

In a clarifying article in the *Review and Herald* two years later, [2]
she made it clear that her astonishing (and, to many, disturbing)
statement did not mean that she was disclaiming the *role* of prophet
("If others call me by that name, I have no controversy with
them"), [3] only the *title* ("I know that many have called me a
prophet, but I have made no claim to this title"). [4]

She had two reasons for not calling herself by the title of prophet:
(1) "because in these days many who boldly claim that they are
prophets are a reproach to the cause of Christ"—a tangential
reference to Joseph Smith (among perhaps others), who died in the
spring of 1844 and whose advocacy of polygamy was a scandal to
many Christians of the day. And (2) "because my work includes
much more than the word 'prophet' signifies." [5]

Ellen White did not want to be considered merely as a "fortuneteller," as a predictor of the future—her work was much broader
than that. But the historical facts are that she did make predictions of
the future. We will consider several, in this and other chapters.

Birth of Modern Spiritualism

Historians of religion in America generally agree that "in the
United States, the modern spiritualist movement began in 1848." [6]
The town was Hydesville, New York, a community situated some 35
miles east of Rochester; [7] the place was the home of the John D. Fox
family. [8]

A peddler reportedly had died in this house sometime earlier, and tenants prior to the occupancy of the Fox family had been repeatedly disturbed by strange noises, particularly the sound of knocking, tapping, or rapping. [9] Two teenage Fox girls, Margaret and Katie, initially were frightened by bedclothes being pulled off the bed, and chairs and tables being removed from their places by invisible hands. They overcame their fears and, somewhat emboldened, eventually managed to develop a code by which they communicated with this alleged "spirit." [10]

Thus modern spiritualism was born!

Ellen White had been receiving messages from God through prophetic visions for about three years now. About a year or less after the "Rochester rappings" had begun, with subsequent widespread publicity, the Lord sent a message to His church through Ellen concerning this new historic development.

On Sabbath, March 24, 1849, in a meeting of Sabbathkeepers at Topsham, Maine, she was told four things about this new phenomenon:

1. *It was satanic in origin.* "I saw that the mysterious knocking in New York and other places was the power of Satan." [11] Four decades later, in an expanded account in *The Great Controversy,* she added:

"The mysterious rapping with which modern spiritualism began was not the result of human trickery or cunning, but was the direct work of evil angels, who thus introduced one of the most successful of soul-destroying delusions. Many will be ensnared through the belief that spiritualism is a merely human imposture; when brought face to face with manifestations which they cannot but regard as supernatural, they will be deceived, and will be led to accept them as the great power of God." [12]

2. *The phenomenon would spread widely and quickly.* In an early account of the 1849 vision Ellen wrote that "such things would be more and more common." [13] What is the testimony of the historians of our own time, looking back at the "Rochester rappings"?

John P. Dever: "This widely advertised event set off a Spiritism revival in the United States that soon spread to England and Europe." [14] F. L. Cross: "Spiritualism . . . soon spread to England and the Continent." [15] And R. S. Ellwood: "A Spiritualist enthusiasm sparked by these revelations swept the country and spread to Europe and Latin America." [16]

3. *The "rappings," though initially a secular phenomenon, would soon also take on a life of their own in the world of religion.* In the earliest days spiritualists would perform their occult arts before bedazzled, dumbfounded audiences in vaudeville and at the circus. *The Academic American Encyclopedia* shares this interesting bit of historical trivia: The Fox sisters performed their arcane arts at séances and toured with the circus of master showman Phineas Taylor Barnum (1810-1891) (best remembered today for his cynical remark "There's a sucker born every minute"). [17] As a result, they "soon became celebrities." [18]

Three Major Denominations

But—as predicted—the secular soon entered the world of religion. Today there are three major "denominations" of spiritualist churches:

a. The International General Assembly of Spiritualists, organized at Buffalo, New York, in 1936 "for the purpose of chartering Spiritualist churches," is today headquartered at Norfolk, Virginia. [19] In 1940 it reported 90 churches, with 1,350 members. [20] In a mere 12 years, by 1952, they had doubled the number of churches to 182, and recorded a membership explosion to 157,000 communicants. [21] (The 1956 membership figure of 164,072 continued to be reported as a static statistic annually until 1977, when church officials discontinued making any data available to the public.) [22]

b. The National Spiritual Alliance of the U.S.A. reported 255 churches, with 4,570 members, in 1936. [23] It fell upon hard times by 1969, with the number of churches dropping to 34, and membership to 3,230. (These figures never changed in annual reports through 1982, when the Alliance, too, discontinued making church records public.) [24] Its self-description during the years of reporting declared that "this body, founded in 1913, believes in supernormal, personal, and impersonal manifestations and in intercommunication between denizens of different worlds." [25] The last known address of their general organization was Keene, New Hampshire.

c. The National Spiritualist Association of Churches continues to style itself as an "organization . . . made up of believers that Spiritualism is a science, philosophy, and religion based upon the demonstrated facts of communication between this world and the next." [26] In 1970 it hit its high-water mark in number of churches: 204, with membership at 5,000 adherents. From 1984 through 1989 it reported 142 churches, with 5,558 members, and 142 clergy. [27]

The last-named denomination, the NSAC, is considered by at least one historian of American religion, John P. Dever, as "the orthodox body of American Spiritualism and the most prominent":

"They maintain a seminary for the training of their ministers. Regular services are held by the churches, and many of the standard religious rituals are observed—singing, praying, etc. This is combined with the practice of mediumship. Camps provide convenient centers for worship, instruction, and practice." [28]

Continuing, Dever summarizes in these words:

"Although the actual membership of the Spiritualist groups in the United States is much less than 200,000 [in 1981], the groups claimed in 1971 that there were over 1,000,000 believers." [29]

(The *Encyclopedia Americana,* on the other hand, listed the high-water mark of organized Spiritualism at a figure in excess of 10 million, based on leadership claims, though it does not specify the year for which this figure was attributed.) [30]

Interestingly, the very existence of descriptive articles in religious dictionaries (such as the *Abingdon Dictionary of Living Religions, Oxford Dictionary of the Christian Church,* and *New International Dictionary of the Christian Church,* among others) is itself mute evidence that spiritualism has become part of the mainstream of world religious movements in our twentieth century. Interestingly, the 1988 edition of the *Encyclopedia Britannica* carries not one but two articles on the subject: one deals with spiritualism in philosophy, while the other (which is nearly three times longer) covers spiritualism in religion!

Certainly Ellen White's prediction that spiritualism would be "clothed in a religious garb" has been amply fulfilled, as also Satan's twofold purpose in producing this metamorphosis to the religious: (a) "to lull the deceived to greater security" and (b) "to draw the minds of God's people, if possible, to those things and cause them to doubt the teachings and power of the Holy Ghost." [31]

4. Finally, Ellen White predicted that *spiritualism would be linked with "mesmerism" or hypnotism.* [32] Says historian Dever, "The Spiritualists draw heavily on the teachings of Emanuel Swedenborg, Franz Mesmer [the German physician who lived from 1734 to

1815 and popularized hypnosis in his practice], and Andrew Jackson Davis." [33]

Swedenborg (1688-1772) can be considered in one sense as a "godfather" to modern spiritualism. Long before its rise, "Swedenborg went into a trancelike state and communed with the spirits, bringing back messages of both practical and religious characters." [34]

As for Mesmer, Stefan Zweig credits him, in *The Three Healers* (1931), with "great contributions" to the Spiritualist movement. Another summarized and synthesized it this way:

"Mesmer and his followers found that the mesmeric or hypnotic trance seemed to bring out certain powers that the normal state did not, and they used these in the diagnosis and treatment of disease. It is no great jump from this practice to that of spirit healing by the entranced medium." [35]

Vision of 1850

Seventeen months to the day after her first vision on modern spiritualism (March 24, 1849), Ellen White received a second, on August 24, 1850. It reiterated the three points of the earlier vision on spiritualism (satanic origin, a quick-spreading phenomenon, and metamorphosis to a religion), and added four new elements:

1. *No criticism would be brooked by the new religion:* "I saw that soon it would be considered blasphemy to speak against the rapping." [36] In 1948 the *Centennial Book of Modern Spiritualism in America* declared:

"Neither priest nor press should uncharitably speak of, or touch this holy word Spiritualism, only with clean hands and pure hearts; and Spiritualists themselves should honor their blessed gospel of immortality." [37]

2. *Increase of satanic miracles:* "I saw . . . that Satan's power would increase and some of his devoted followers would have power to work miracles, and even to bring down fire from heaven in the sight of men." [38]

Even the staid, conservative *Oxford Dictionary of the Christian Church* is impressed:

"After ruling out conscious or unconscious fraud, of which almost all famous mediums have been convicted, and phenomena susceptible of a natural explanation, e.g., by the abnormal qualities of the medium, there remains a certain number of striking cases such as the foreseeing of free actions and otherwise incalculable events." [39]

In the *Encyclopedia Americana* the late Dr. Joseph B. Rhine (1895-1980), founder/director of Duke University's respected Institute for Parapsychology, responded also in serious tone: "The question raised by Spiritualism must be faced as one of science's greatest problems." [40]

3. *Jesus' miracles credited to spiritualism:* Said Ellen further:

"I was shown that by the rapping and mesmerism these modern magicians would yet account for all the miracles wrought by our Lord Jesus Christ, and that many would believe that all the mighty works of the Son of God when on earth were accomplished by this same power." [41]

Again, hear from the *Centennial Book of Modern Spiritualism in America:*

"A medium foretold the birth of Jesus, whose brief life on earth was filled with the performance of many so-called miracles which in reality were spiritual phenomena." [42]

4. Finally, *Ellen White made a prediction that,* if not already fulfilled, *will undoubtedly come to fruition* in the comparatively near future:

"I was pointed back to the time of Moses and saw the signs and wonders which God wrought through him before Pharaoh, most of which were imitated by the magicians of Egypt; and that just before the final deliverance of the saints, God would work powerfully for His people, and these modern magicians would be permitted to imitate the work of God." [43]

Further Counsel in 1854

Four years after her second vision dealing with spiritualism (1850), Ellen White wrote "An Explanation" to clarify and amplify some of her earlier statements relative to the visions of 1849 and 1850 on this subject.

She started out by stating that many of the things shown in 1849 had now, five years later, already been fulfilled "beyond the expectations of anyone." [44]

Then she went into a detailed plea for Seventh-day Adventists not to allow their minds to be "taken up with the things around us," but rather to be "occupied with the present truth and a preparation to give a reason of our hope with meekness and fear." [45]

Specifically, Adventists were in dire need of "a thorough understanding of present truth, which they will be obliged to maintain from the Scriptures. They must understand the state of the dead; for the spirits of devils will yet appear to them, professing to be beloved friends and relatives, who will declare to them that the Sabbath has been changed, also other unscriptural doctrines. They will do all in their power to excite sympathy and will work miracles before them to confirm what they declare." [46]

Ellen White foretold that Satan's evil angels would impersonate the apostles and other writers of Scripture (as well as ordinary persons) and cause them to declare that what they had written in the Bible was in error. Now allegedly on "the other side," they have "learned better." They claim that what they wrote in the Bible was "adulterated," and that Christians should now listen to these *spirits* of the departed patriarchs and prophets rather than to follow what they wrote anciently in the Word of God: [47]

"The apostles, as personated by these lying spirits, are made to contradict what they wrote at the dictation of the Holy Spirit when on earth. They deny the divine origin of the Bible, and thus tear away the foundation of the Christian's hope and put out the light that reveals the way to heaven. Satan is making the world believe that the Bible is a mere fiction, or at least a book suited to the infancy of the race, but now to be lightly regarded, or cast aside as obsolete." [48]

"Train of Cars" Metaphor

In one of her most memorable metaphors, Ellen White describes something that she saw in a "parable" vision. The date is not specified, but it was sometime between the vision of 1850 and the writing of this description in 1854:

"I saw the rapidity with which this delusion was spreading. A train of cars was shown me, going with the speed of lightning. The angel bade me look carefully. I fixed my eyes upon the train. It seemed that the whole world was on board, that there could not be one left. Said the angel, 'They are binding in bundles ready to burn.' Then he showed me the conductor, who appeared like a stately, fair person, whom all the passengers looked up to and reverenced. I was perplexed and asked my attending angel who it was. He said, 'It is Satan. He is the conductor in the form of an angel of light. He has taken the world captive. They are given over to strong delusions, to believe a lie, that they may be damned. This agent, the next highest in order to him, is the engineer, and other of his agents are employed in different offices as he may need them, and they are all going with lightning speed to perdition.' "

Ellen plaintively inquired if there were none left, and the angel told her to look in the opposite direction. "And I saw a little company traveling a narrow pathway. All seemed to be firmly united, bound together by the truth, in bundles, or companies. Said the angel, 'The third angel is binding, or sealing, them in bundles for the heavenly garner.' This little company looked careworn, as if they had passed through severe trials and conflicts. And it appeared as if the sun had just risen from behind a cloud and shone upon their countenances, causing them to look triumphant, as if their victories were nearly won." [49]

Spiritualism Today

The craze in spiritualism in the 1990s is the New Age phenomenon known as channeling. In it the human medium gives over his or her body and vocal mechanism to a spirit, to proclaim messages from some long-departed "person."

J. Z. Knight, 40, a housewife from Yelm, Washington, allowed "Ramtha"—alleged to be a 35,000-year-old man—to speak through her to 400 persons over the Thanksgiving holiday in 1986, at the Doubletree Plaza Hotel outside Seattle. Each person attending the seminar paid $400 for the privilege! [50]

Whereas the audiences for these modern soothsayers until recently were about 90 percent housewives, now they are approximately 60 percent business and professional people.

In January 1987 the American Broadcasting Company devoted five hours of prime-time television to actress Shirley MacLaine's "personal trek through a psychic world." She had already sold 4 million copies of one of her two "mystic experience" books; after that exposure on television both books hit the best-selling charts again.

A University of Chicago poll in 1986 demonstrated that 67 percent of the public claims to have had at least one psychic experience. [51]

Ellen G. White's "Spirit" Returns!

I do not know that Ellen White ever predicted that her own "spirit" would return after her death, though she clearly (and repeatedly) affirmed that evil spirits would impersonate the writers of the Bible to contradict what they had stated in the Scriptures. But in 1974 one of the three most famous women writers on psychic phenomena, Ruth Montgomery, declared that she had received a message from Ellen White in the great beyond!

The story is a fascinating one: In that year (1974) Nicholas Steubing, a new convert to Seventh-day Adventism from the world of the occult, wanted to do some missionary work among the writers who had substantially influenced his life in the world of spiritualism. So he sent Ruth Montgomery a letter, together with a gift copy of *The Great Controversy.*

Montgomery has written 11 books on various aspects of the occult, published between 1965 and 1983. Most of them enjoyed popular sales in the multimillion-copy bracket. [52]

On April 17, 1974, when she was well on her way to fame, Ruth Montgomery replied to Steubing in a personal, hand-signed letter that read:

"Dear Nicholas Steubing:

"Thanks so very much for sending *The Great Controversy* to me. I am reading it with interest, and it was most generous of you to think of me in this respect. She certainly is prejudiced against the Catholics, isn't she—glad I was reared a Methodist!

"Oddly enough, in the automatic writing session this morning the Guides brought me a communication that said, 'The woman White who wrote the book you are reading is here and says: Please, please disregard what I wrote about communication with the living dead.'

"I do thank you from the heart.

"Sincerely,

"[signed] Ruth Montgomery" [53]

Crowning Counterfeit

In *The Great Controversy* Ellen White speaks of "the crowning act in the great drama of deception" at the end of time when Satan will impersonate Christ in an attempted counterfeit of the Second

Coming. Her description leaves one in no doubt as to whether or not Mrs. White herself witnessed this in vision:

"In different parts of the earth, Satan will manifest himself as a majestic being of dazzling brightness, resembling the description of the Son of God given by John in the Revelation [1:13-15]. The glory that surrounds him is unsurpassed by anything that mortal eyes have yet beheld. . . . His voice is soft and subdued, yet full of melody. In gentle, compassionate tones he presents some of the same gracious, heavenly truths which the Saviour uttered; he heals the diseases of the people, and then, in his assumed character of Christ, he claims to have changed the Sabbath to Sunday, and commands all to hallow the day which he has blessed. . . . This is the strong, almost overmastering delusion." [54]

It is to this event that Mrs. White applies the prediction of Jesus that, if it were possible, Satan would deceive the "very elect" (Matt. 24:24). And she points out that Christians will be able to detect the counterfeit only by the objective word of God; if they rely upon subjective human senses, they will surely be lost, so coercive will the evidence become:

1. Satan contradicts what the Bible teaches concerning the sacredness and sanctity of the seventh-day Sabbath, and places a blessing upon that group—possessors of the mark of the beast—that receives the ultimate curse of Scripture!

2. The Bible declares that when Jesus returns we will meet Him in the sky, not on the earth (1 Thess. 4:17)—whereas Satan will be walking in different parts of this earth. Satan will not be permitted to counterfeit the physical manner of the Second Coming. [55]

Conclusion

Between 1849 and 1858 Ellen White made at least 10 major observations concerning the origin, rise, growth, development, and direction of modern spiritualism:

1. The "Rochester rappings" of Hydesville, New York, which launched modern spiritualism in 1848, were "the direct work of evil spirits."

2. They would spread widely and rapidly.

3. Though initially a secular phenomenon, they would soon metamorphose into a religious movement.

4. The movement would link up with hypnosis, both coming from a common source.

5. No criticism would be brooked by the new religion.

6. There would be a marked, continuing increase in satanic miracles.

7. The miracles of Jesus would be dismissed as merely spiritualistic operations.

8. These miracles would become a major factor in the end-time scenario.

9. Evil angels would impersonate the writers of the Bible, ostensibly now returning from the spirit world to correct alleged "errors" in their writings, on the basis of additional new information gained on "the other side."

10. The "crowning act" of the great controversy end-time drama will be Satan's attempt to impersonate Christ in a counterfeit second coming.

Ellen White sounds this solemn warning to all who live in the end-time:

"Only those who have been diligent students of the Scriptures and who have received the love of the truth will be shielded from the powerful delusion that takes the world captive. By the Bible testimony these will detect the deceiver in his disguise. To all the testing time will come. . . .

"Satan will, if possible, prevent them from obtaining a preparation to stand in that day. He will so arrange affairs as to hedge up their way, entangle them with earthly treasures, cause them to carry a heavy, wearisome burden, that their hearts may be overcharged with the cares of this life and the day of trial may come upon them as a thief." [56]

May he have no success with you, my friend!

Notes and References

[1] 1SM 32, note.

[2] RH, July 26, 1906; cited in 1SM 31-36.

[3] 1SM 34.

[4] *Ibid.*, p. 32.

[5] *Ibid.*

[6] "Spiritualism," *World Book Encyclopedia* (1990), vol. 18, p. 796.

[7] EW, 5th ed. (1963) 300, appendix note, "Mysterious Knockings in New York, and Rochester Rappings."

[8] "Spiritism," *The New International Dictionary of the Christian Church*, rev. ed. (1981), p. 926.

[9] "Spiritualism, Spiritism," *Abingdon Dictionary of Living Religions* (1981), p. 713.

[10] "Spiritism," p. 926.

[11] EW 43.

[12] GC 553.

[13] EW 43.

[14] "Spiritism," p. 926.

[15] "Spiritualism," *The Oxford Dictionary of the Christian Church,* p. 1283.

[16] "Spiritualism, Spiritism," p. 713.

[17] John Bartlett, *Familiar Quotations,* 14th ed. (1980), p. 536.

[18] *Academic American Encyclopedia* (1983), vol. 18, p. 189.

[19] *Yearbook of American and Canadian Churches* (1976), p. 67.

[20] *Ibid.* (1941).

[21] *Ibid.* (1953).

[22] *Ibid.* (1958; 1977).

[23] *Ibid.* (1941).

[24] *Ibid.* (1982).

[25] *Ibid.* (1976).

[26] *Ibid.*

[27] *Ibid.* (1973; 1974; 1989).

[28] "Spiritism," p. 926.

[29] *Ibid.*

[30] "Spiritualism," *Encyclopedia Americana* (1983), vol. 25, p. 515.

[31] EW 43.

[32] *Ibid.,* p. 44.

[33] "Spiritism," p. 926.

[34] "Spiritualism," *Encyclopedia Americana,* p. 515.

[35] *Ibid.*

[36] EW 59.

[37] *Centennial Book of Modern Spiritualism in America* (Chicago: National Spiritualist Association of United States of America, 1948), p. 34.

[38] EW 59.

[39] "Spiritualism," *Oxford Dictionary,* p. 1283.

[40] "Spiritualism," *Encyclopedia Americana,* p. 516.

[41] EW 59.

[42] Centennial, p. 68.

[43] EW 59, 60.

[44] *Ibid.,* p. 86.

[45] *Ibid.,* p. 87.

[46] *Ibid.*

[47] *Ibid.,* p. 90.

[48] GC 557.

[49] EW 88, 89.

[50] "And Now, the 35,000-Year-Old Man," *Time,* Dec. 15, 1986, p. 36; "Ramtha, a Voice From Beyond," *Newsweek,* Dec. 15, 1986, p. 42.

[51] "Mystics on Main Street," *U.S. News & World Report,* Feb. 9, 1987, pp. 67-69.

[52] A list of *all* of Ruth Montgomery's published works appears in the biographical sketch "Ruth Shick Montgomery," *Who's Who in America,* 45th ed. (1988-1989), p. 2190.

[53] Written at Cuernavaca, Mexico, from a photocopy of the original letter.

[54] GC 624, 625.

[55] *Ibid.,* p. 625.

[56] *Ibid.,* pp. 625, 626.

CHAPTER 5

THE GREAT CONTROVERSY VISION
"The Theme"

March 14, 1858

A RE you sufficiently familiar with the writings of Ellen White
that if asked which is your favorite book you would have a
ready answer? For many Seventh-day Adventists, the number
one favorite would probably be *Steps to Christ,* followed closely
perhaps by *The Desire of Ages.*

Which of all her writings would Mrs. White herself choose? She
never gave a direct answer, but concerning *The Great Controversy*
she did make two revealing statements. In a 1911 letter to Francis M.
Wilcox, several months after he assumed the editorship of the
Review and Herald, Ellen wrote, "The book *The Great Controversy*
I appreciate above silver or gold, and I greatly desire that it shall
come before the people." [1]

In 1905, six years earlier, she had declared to Drs. Daniel and
Lauretta Kress, then serving in Australia and New Zealand, "I am
more anxious to see a wide circulation for this book than for any
others I have written." [2]

One instinctively wonders, Why this book?

In various statements penned between 1890 and 1911 she
mentioned various reasons for her preference:

• "While writing the manuscript . . . I was often conscious of the
presence of the angels of God" [3]; and those same "angels of God
would prepare the way for these books in the hearts of the people." [4]

• "In *The Great Controversy,* the last message of warning to the
world is given more distinctly than in any of my other books," [5] and
"these books contain God's direct appeal to the people. . . . They are

the voice of God speaking to His people and they will have an influence upon minds that other books do not have." [6]

• She deemed this book "especially adapted to those who have newly come to the faith, that they may be established in the truth." [7]

• "The Holy Spirit traced these truths upon my heart and mind as indelibly as the law was traced by the finger of God, upon the tables of stone, which are now in the ark." [8]

• "The Lord has declared that these books are to be scattered throughout the world." [9]

One looks in vain among her writings, however, to find another deeply emotional reason, perhaps withheld because of self-consciousness: *Because this book very nearly cost her her life—* literally! The story of the background circumstances of this vision is almost as exciting as the far-reaching content of the vision itself.

Visit to Northwest Ohio

The year was 1858.

James and Ellen White had moved two years previously from Rochester, New York, to Battle Creek, Michigan. As yet, the very first steps in formal church organization of the movement they were spearheading—choosing a corporate name and establishing a publishing house—were still two years distant. But the work of the movement was growing, and it required the personal attention of these two chief leaders. And that meant frequent travel.

The Whites were also parents, and in the spring of 1858 three young sons were at home: Henry, 10; Edson, 8; and little Willie, nearly 4. These were being cared for right in their own home by two young women who boarded there for that purpose. The Whites themselves prepared to leave on a three-stop itinerary of northwest Ohio, scheduled for late February to mid-March. [10]

A news note in the *Review and Herald,* February 18 issue, informed its readers that the Whites would attend a "conference of the commandment keepers of Ohio" at Green Spring the weekend of February 26-28. Another conference at Gilboa would be held the following weekend, March 6 and 7. (A final weekend, at Lovett's Grove, March 13 and 14, was not mentioned in this particular press announcement.)

James and Ellen arrived at the Green Spring depot of the

Sandusky City & Indiana Railroad, the village's first rail link with Ohio (opened only four years earlier). They were met by a "Bro. and Sr. Tillotson," who provided transportation in their "comfortable" carriage for the 18-day, 120-mile circle-trip from Green Spring to Gilboa to Lovett's Grove to Fremont.[11] The Tillotsons, apparently "new converts," [12] may possibly be linked with a "Charles O. Tillotson" listed 11 years later in the county directory as a "vessel owner" resident in Fremont.[13] (At that time the Sandusky River was navigable from Lake Erie as far south as Fremont.)

Green Springs (sometime during the past century an "s" was added to the town's name) today is a hamlet of nearly 1,600, situated nine miles southeast of Fremont, where the Whites subsequently ended their two-and-one-half-week odyssey.

Surveyed in 1839 (and first called Stem Town, after its founder), nine years before the Whites came to call, its chief claim to fame then, as now, was its possession of the "world's largest natural sulphur springs"—hence the current name. It is part of Adams Township, which is bisected by the boundary line between Sandusky and Seneca counties.

There were probably several hundred inhabitants in Green Spring when the Whites arrived in 1858 (the population in 1840 was 29, but by 1900 it had risen to about 1,000).[14]

Adventism in Green Spring

Seventh-day Adventist views were first introduced into Green Spring by Joseph Bates in October 1853. Seeking out ex-Millerites who had lost interest following the Great Disappointment, Bates spoke in a public hall, and the whole town turned out. Two months later J. N. Loughborough followed up with a series of five meetings in a schoolhouse. At the final Sunday night service there was standing room only inside; many listened from outside, with ears pressed against windows.[15]

Green Spring was nothing if not religious; when the Whites arrived in 1858, Adams Township boasted seven active churches[16] in addition to the little company of Adventist believers. (They formally organized themselves into a church four years later, in 1862.)[17]

But the reception accorded James White's preaching in Green Spring left much to be desired, as he himself indicated with some apparent disappointment in the *Review and Herald:*

"We preached at this meeting the best we could, but it was a dark hard place to preach. Some who had been in the truth for years came with an exalted spirit, destitute of a sense of the solemnity of this time and the present work. The erring were faithfully reproved. The meeting closed with some degree of freedom, and hope for better times in time to come." [18]

Although the meetings closed on Sunday, the Whites remained in Green Spring until at least Wednesday, March 3, staying in the home of a family of new converts named Sharp.

While here, Ellen received two visions and wrote three letters. The first vision concerned the spiritual condition of Mary, wife of leader J. N. Loughborough. In a long letter (seven pages in typewritten form; of course, she wrote by hand) Ellen pleaded with Mary to surrender a stubborn will to Jesus, and not to continue attempting to dominate her husband. Pointedly she wrote: "Mary, your will has often pulled John one way, when God directed him in another.... Do not drive him to regret his choice [in making you his wife]." [19]

The second vision revealed "the wretched state of things [among Seventh-day Adventists] in New York," especially in Oswego County, and prompted a letter to a "Brother Woodruff," suggesting ways of dealing with the "wrangling and strife" in his church there. [20]

The final letter was addressed to her two eldest boys, and told of a mother's aching heart longing for their childish prattle. It urged faithfulness in study and home duties, special care for little Willie; and thoughtful, helpful kindnesses to "sisters Jennie and Martha," who cared for them temporarily as surrogate parents. [21]

Problems at Gilboa

Some time on Thursday or Friday (March 4 or 5), the Tillotsons took the Whites to Gilboa, some 50 miles southwest of Green Spring. Town historian Margarete Conine reports that Gilboa was the first town settled in Putnam County; it possessed three churches and seven taverns when the Whites visited in 1858. [22]

All three local churches "were closed against us," refusing to allow "Advent" meetings within their precincts; so a small schoolroom (50 feet by 25 feet) was booked. Some 100 Sabbathkeepers and curious townspeople crowded in. "The place was very uncomfortable," James White reported, but he was most gratified that their weekend attendance exceeded that of all three inhospitable local churches combined!

With perhaps a fleeting nod in the direction of Gilboa's taverns, White declared that "the opposition in Gilboa is bold and wicked." Even so, he added:

"We had freedom in speaking the Word, but our feelings were saddened at the bold, scoffing faces of many scorners. The pointed, solemn truth spoken sometimes caused even the scoffer to weep, but he would next moment resist it with a careless smile, or cover his feelings with a sort of angry grin." [23]

James was thrilled that 80 believers were professing "present truth." He was moved to declare optimistically, "The harvest is very ripe in Gilboa." [24]

During their conference at Gilboa, the brethren proceeded with the ordination to the gospel ministry, "by prayer and the laying on of hands," of T. J. Butler, a local resident. [25] This is significant in that the formal organization of the Seventh-day Adventist denomination was still two years distant.

Butler managed to distinguish himself at the organizing conference at Battle Creek, October 1, 1860. He was the only delegate who registered dissent to the adoption of the corporate name "Seventh-day Adventist." He favored "Church of God," in spite of Mrs. White's support for the Seventh-day Adventist label. (Four other delegates, perhaps equally dubious, merely abstained from voting at all.) He also opposed a motion to recommend the Seventh-day Adventist name to "the churches generally." [26] Both motions passed overwhelmingly, however.

Visit to Lovett's Grove

Sometime between Monday, March 8, and Friday, March 12, the Tillotsons and the Whites made their way 35 miles north of Gilboa to a hamlet called Lovett's Grove (after a well-known local grove of black walnut trees). At that time Lovett's Grove and nearby Bowling Green, two miles to the south, were competing for supremacy in local municipal growth and status; Lovett's Grove had its own post office and other amenities. Today it is just a wide spot in the road on U.S. Route 25.

The visitors found there a new company of some 40 Sabbath-keepers, recently raised up through the evangelistic prowess of

George W. Holt. James White later wrote, "We enjoyed great freedom with these brethren." [27]

(On February 8, 1862, the Lovett's Grove company became the first Seventh-day Adventist church to organize in Ohio. [28] A bronze marker, jointly sponsored by the Wood County and Ohio State historical societies, commemorates the event.)

In reporting that "on First-day God manifested His power in a wonderful manner," James White apparently referred to the response to his call to become a member of the Advent band. He wrote that "several decided to keep the Lord's Sabbath and go with the people of God." [29]

Incredibly, however, White omits any reference whatever to the most dramatic exhibition of God's power—his wife's subsequent vision, which substantially interrupted the funeral service he conducted that Sunday afternoon in the local schoolhouse!

For two hours [30] Ellen was given a two-part message by God. As so often happened on similar occasions, there was revealed specific, practical counsel to meet immediate problems and needs of the local congregation. Then there was given a more broad message for the church at large, this time a cosmic sweep of the ages-long war "between Christ and His angels, and Satan and his angels" (as she later characterized it in a rather lengthy formal book title typical of the day).

Locally, members with unbelieving spouses and children were urged to patience and forbearance if their lot were, ultimately, to "walk the straight path alone." Yet they should "never indulge a harsh, unkind spirit. . . . Treat them tenderly. Give them no occasion to reproach the cause of Christ; but never yield the truth to please anyone. Be decided, be fixed, be established, be not of a doubtful mind.

"But if your companions and children will not come, if you cannot win them to yield to the claims of truth, make their lives here as pleasant as possible; for all they will ever enjoy will be this poor world." [31]

With regard to the broader subject, Ellen White had been given a more limited view of this great controversy theme some 10 years earlier. What, then, was different this time? (1) Now she was given a much more greatly expanded, detailed view of the issues and events; (2) now she was told, for the first time, to write it all out; and (3) now she was bluntly warned by God that "I should have to contend with the powers of darkness, for Satan would make strong efforts to hinder me, but angels of God would not leave me in the conflict, that in God I must put my trust." [32]

Little did she or James realize how quickly—and in what startling manner—the attack of Satan would take place!

The Curtain Lifted

God's prophets were called "seers" before they were called "prophets" (1 Sam. 9:9), because prophets "see" things that prophetically ungifted persons do not. As Ellen so eloquently put it in another of her books dealing with the great controversy theme:

"In the annals of human history, the growth of nations, the rise and fall of empires, appear as if dependent on the will and prowess of man; the shaping of events seems, to a great degree, to be determined by his power, ambition, or caprice. But in the Word of God the curtain is drawn aside, and we behold, above, behind, and through all the play and counterplay of human interests and power and passions, the agencies of the All-merciful One, silently, patiently working out the counsels of His own will." [33]

Nor were the Bible prophets the only ones privileged to look behind the veil. In her introduction to *The Great Controversy* (and it was *her* introduction, contrary to some contemporary critics; in a letter to Dr. David Paulson she twice uses the singular personal pronoun in referring to "my introduction" and "my statement"), [34] Ellen claimed possession of supernatural information:

"Through the illumination of the Holy Spirit, the scenes of the long-continued conflict between good and evil have been opened to the writer of these pages. From time to time I have been permitted to behold the working, in different ages, of the great controversy between Christ, the Prince of life, the Author of our salvation, and Satan, the prince of evil, the author of sin, the first transgressor of God's holy law. . . .

"As the Spirit of God has opened to my mind the great truths of His Word, and the scenes of the past and the future, I have been bidden to make known to others that which has thus been revealed—to trace the history of the controversy in past ages, and especially so to present it as to shed a light on the fast-approaching struggle of the future." [35]

After Ellen came out of vision, the funeral finally concluded with the long-delayed interment of the deceased by mourning relatives and friends. Ellen later remembered, "Great solemnity rested upon those who remained";[36] and as all then went to their homes, the murmur reportedly could be heard in awe-stricken tones, "We have seen strange things today." [37]

On Monday, March 15, the Tillotsons took the Whites in their carriage the 30 miles from Lovett's Grove to Fremont (where the hosts are believed to have lived), a good day's journey in those days by horse-drawn conveyance, even over good roads. There the Whites remained overnight, presumably in the Tillotson home, until their rail departure for Michigan the next day. [38]

When the Whites entered Fremont that Monday evening they did not know that one of the town's lawyers, 36-year-old Rutherford B. Hayes, would 10 years later be elected governor of the state of Ohio, nor that in 1877 he would become the nineteenth president of the United States.

But they may have heard about Fort Stephenson, the remnants of which were still somewhat in evidence there. On August 1-3, 1813, a decisive battle had been fought at this fort in Fremont (then called Lower Sandusky) that tipped the scales of the War of 1812 in favor of the Americans.

The exploits of 21-year-old George Croghan during the battle were still the talk of the town. With only 160 Americans he had spectacularly routed a vastly superior force of 1,500 Indian and British forces under Tecumseh and Henry Proctor. The army of William Henry Harrison in the West was thereby saved, making possible a later victory at the Thames in Ontario. This effectively ended the war in victory for the American forces.

Having just seen in vision Christ's ultimate victory (against great odds and after a prolonged siege) over Satan and his natural and supernatural forces, Ellen doubtless would have cherished—even relished—the story of young Croghan's victory as she retired to her bed that night.

Return to Michigan

On Tuesday, March 16, the Tillotsons said their final goodbyes to the Whites at the Fremont railroad depot, where the latter boarded the train for a 170-mile trip to Jackson, Michigan.

Just how much had been said between the Tillotsons and the Whites in the carriage during their daylong journey on Monday, with reference to the content of Ellen's vision the previous afternoon, is not known.

But now alone for the first time since the magnificent Sunday afternoon revelation, James and Ellen spent the whole day in talking about, and laying careful plans for, the writing and publishing of the book that the angel had commissioned. Work began immediately upon their return home.

Satan and his angels are as dependent as you and I when it comes to discerning the future, for they do not themselves possess the gift of prophetic inspiration. They must depend solely upon the utterances of the prophets, as do we. Therefore, Satan takes great pains to determine the identity of God's true prophets. Then he hounds their footsteps to become the first to learn the specifics of the content of their visions and revelations.

It is not at all unlikely that Satan and his evil angels—along with God's holy guardian angels, of course—were the first to read the words of the book of Daniel as the aged prophet wrote his scroll "by the waters of Babylon." And the forces of evil doubtless kibitzed over the shoulder of the apostle John as he penned the Revelation on the lonely slopes of the Isle of Patmos. For they have a vested interest in learning what the future holds—the better to plan their strategy of counterattack.

Thus it is not at all improbable that Satan was a nonpaying "passenger" in that railroad coach March 16, 1858, hovering above the Whites as the train made its way westward to Jackson. It is equally likely that when he learned the devastating extent to which God had revealed the future and exposed the devil's modus operandi, that he urgently realized the need to act—quickly—to keep that book from ever being written, if possible.

Because of train schedules it was likely necessary for the Whites to spend Tuesday night in Jackson, and then to board another train Wednesday morning for the remaining 40 miles to their final destination, Battle Creek. Meeting them at the Jackson railway station to provide overnight hospitality were old friends Daniel and Abigail Palmer, with their carriage.

Palmer was a blacksmith, the first Seventh-day Adventist convert (with David Hewitt) of Joseph Bates in the state of Michigan.[39] He was also a longtime friend of the Whites. As he took them to his residence at 1705 East Main Street (now East Michigan Avenue), a mile or two from the depot, they doubtless passed his blacksmith forge on the north side of Main, near Van Dorn.

James and Ellen had been in the Palmer house four years earlier. The house looms large in significance in the history of Adventism in Michigan. Four important events had transpired within its walls before this fateful night of March 16, 1858:

1852: Joseph Bates had here converted a first-day Adventist pastor, M. E. Cornell, when the latter dropped in for a visit en route to a new parish elsewhere. (Cornell, in turn, converted John P. Kellogg, father of Dr. John Harvey, and Cornell's in-laws, parents of his wife, Angeline Lyon Cornell!) [40]

1853: Hiram S. Case and C. P. Russell were here rebuked for unchristian behavior toward certain laymen, whereupon they promptly defected to start the *Messenger* party, the first Seventh-day Adventist offshoot movement. [41]

1854: A council meeting was held here in which the decision was taken to purchase an evangelistic tent for use in Battle Creek—Adventism's first in Michigan. M. E. Cornell left the meeting abruptly to catch a train to New York to make the purchase. [42]

1854: A solemn prayer meeting was held here just prior to the departure of James and Ellen White for a rail trip to Wisconsin. Shortly after the train left the station it derailed, injuring many; the Whites, however, miraculously escaped unscathed! [43]

Now, as they gathered again in these familiar surroundings, perhaps old memories revived. But they could not know that what was about to happen this very night would effectively put all that went before into the shade!

Satan Strikes in Jackson

James White and Daniel Palmer may have been visiting in one room while Ellen and Abigail were in another when, suddenly, as Ellen later recalled:

"My tongue refused to utter what I wished to say, and seemed large and numb. A strange, cold sensation struck my heart, passed over my head, and down my right side. For a while I was insensible; but was aroused by the voice of earnest prayer. I tried to use my left arm and limb, but they were perfectly useless. For a short time I did not expect to live. It was the third shock I had received of paralysis [at age 30], and although within 50 miles of home, I did not expect to see my children again." [44]

Ellen resigned herself to die, thinking that probably her work for the Lord was now at an end. But as her husband and friends continued praying over her prostrate form, "[I] soon [felt] a prickling sensation . . . in my arm and limb, and I praised the Lord that I could use them a little. The Lord had heard the faithful prayers of His children, and the power of Satan was broken." [45]

Ellen was not totally healed, however, and doubtless passed a most difficult night. The next morning she felt "strengthened" to endure the remaining 40 miles home to Battle Creek. "For several weeks I could not feel the pressure of the hand, nor the coldest water poured upon my head. In rising to walk, I often staggered, and sometimes fell to the floor." [46]

It was in this crippled condition that Ellen began to write her book, for the angel had bade her, "Write it out." She trusted again that what God had commanded He would enable her to perform.

Trying to hold a pen one day, she discovered that she could compose but one page of text and then had to have total rest for the next three days! "But as I progressed, my strength increased." And, more important, "the numbness in my head did not seem to becloud my mind, and before I closed that work, the effect of the shock had entirely left me." [47]

It took five months, from mid-March to mid-August, for Ellen to complete her manuscript. In printed form it occupied some 219 pages. Included was a 12-page preface, "Spiritual Gifts," by Roswell F. Cottrell. A news note on the back page of the September 9, 1858, issue of the *Review and Herald* announced to its readers that the book was now available for public sale. [48]

Book Title Chosen

The idea for the title of her book probably came from a work similarly titled: *The Great Controversy Between God and Man: Its Origin, Progress, and Termination,* authored and published by H. L. Hastings of Rochester, New York. A copy of the book had been sent to the Review and Herald publishing office in the hope that its presence would generate a book review in the columns of the *Review.*

That hope was not to be disappointed; in the March 18, 1858, edition it appeared at the top of the final page.

A comparison by Warren H. Johns of these two books with near-identical titles demonstrates the existence of substantial differences between them as regards "scope, purpose, and content." [49]

Both exploit the (by then) well-worn motif of a war between good and evil, perhaps best popularized by the English Puritan poet and political writer John Milton. *Paradise Lost* (1667) is considered by many to be the greatest epic poem ever written in the English language. [50] It was inevitable that similarities of flavor—and even of verbiage—should surround subsequent literary efforts, for, as the wise man had written three millennia earlier, "There is no new thing under the sun" (Eccl. 1:9).

Through the next 40 years Ellen's little 219-page book of 1858 was expanded by its author through two more reincarnations. It finally appeared as the five-volume Conflict of the Ages Series, with only the fifth and final book bearing the original, all-inclusive title *The Great Controversy.*

Patriarchs and Prophets (1890, 754 pages), *Prophets and Kings* (1917, 733 pages), *The Desire of Ages* (1898, 835 pages), *The Acts of the Apostles* (1911, 602 pages), and *The Great Controversy* (1911, 678 pages)—a total of 3,602 pages—all grew from that earlier 219-page book, *Spiritual Gifts,* volume 1!

A Final Note

In June 1858, with the manuscript for *The Great Controversy* about half completed, Ellen White was called away from her writing one day to attend the bedside of a Sister A. S. Hutchins, who was seriously ill and believed near death. While praying for her, Ellen was taken off in vision, during which her angel shared some interesting facts:

"I was shown that in the sudden attack at Jackson, Satan designed to take my life to hinder the work I was about to write; but angels of God were sent to my rescue, to raise me above the effects of Satan's attack. I saw, among other things, that I should be blest with better health than before the attack at Jackson." [51]

For good measure, God raised up Sister Hutchins as a result of Ellen's prayer!

This news should have come as no surprise to Ellen—nor to us.

For while Satan hates all of the prophets with a passion—they, after all, expose the wiles of this "roaring lion" who rampages among Christians, "seeking whom he may devour" (1 Peter 5:8)—he especially hates apocalyptic-writing prophets, who particularly expose his depredations and demise in the end-time.

It is a matter of record that Satan attempted to have Daniel killed in a Persian den of hungry lions, doubtless to prevent the book of Daniel from being written (Dan. 6). Likewise, Daniel's counterpart in the New Testament, John the Beloved, was thrown into a vat of boiling oil, at the order of Roman emperor Domitian (instigated, doubtless, by the devil, again probably to keep the Revelation from being written).

But just as Daniel was preserved from hungry lions, and just as John "was removed [unhurt] from the caldron by the very men who had cast him in," [52] just so was Ellen's life preserved from the malicious attack of Satan in 1858. She had work to do; God wanted a special book to be written!

Is it any wonder, then, that Ellen White appreciated *The Great Controversy* "above silver or gold," and that she desired for this book a greater circulation than for any other of her literary works!

Notes and References

[1] CM 128.

[2] *Ibid.,* p. 127.

[3] *Ibid.,* p. 128.

[4] *Ibid.,* p. 124.

[5] *Ibid.,* p. 127.

[6] *Ibid.,* p. 129.

[7] *Ibid.*

[8] *Ibid.,* p. 126.

[9] *Ibid.,* p. 125.

[10] Letter 3, 1858.

[11] RH, Mar. 25, 1858; 2SG 265, 271.

[12] 1Bio 367; regrettably Arthur W. White provides here no documentation to support such an identification.

[13] *Sandusky County Gazetteer and Directory for 1869* (Sandusky, Ohio: A. Bailey, 1869), p. 49. In 3Index 2813 Tillotson is identified by the given-name initial of J. I am unaware of any extant documentation to support such a characterization.

[14] *Green Springs, Ohio, Centennial, 1872-1972* (Green Springs, Ohio: Green Springs Echo, 1972), pp. 7ff.

[15] SDAE 1020.

[16] *Centennial,* pp. 39-45.

[17] SDAE 1021.

[18] RH, Mar. 25, 1858.

[19] Letter 1, 1858.

[20] Letter 2, 1858.

[21] Letter 3, 1858.

[22] Interview with Margarete Conine, Gilboa town historian, at Gilboa, Ohio, May 25, 1984.

[23] RH, Mar. 25, 1858.

[24] *Ibid.*

[25] *Ibid.*

[26] RH, Oct. 23, 1860.

[27] RH, Mar. 25, 1858.

[28] SDAE 1021.

[29] RH, Mar. 25, 1858.

[30] William C. White, "A View of the Age-Long Conflict," RH, Feb. 20, 1936.

[31] 2SG 266.

[32] *Ibid.,* p. 270.

[33] PK 499, 500.

[34] 1SM 24, 25.

[35] GC x, xi.

[36] 2SG 271.

[37] William C. White, p. 6.

[38] 2SG 271.

[39] Arthur W. Spalding, *Origin and History of Seventh-day Adventists* (Washington, D.C.: Review and Herald Pub. Assn., 1961), vol. 1, p. 223.

[40] *Ibid.,* pp. 219, 220.

[41] *Ibid.,* pp. 229, 252, 253.

[42] *Ibid.,* pp. 265, 266.

[43] LS 153; cf. 2SG 189.

[44] 2SG 271.

[45] *Ibid.,* pp. 271, 272.

[46] *Ibid.,* p. 272.

[47] *Ibid.,* pp. 270, 272.

[48] 1Bio 374.

[49] Warren H. Johns, "Literary Thief or God's Messenger?" *Ministry,* June 1982, pp. 13, 14; cf. Ronald D. Graybill, "The Power of Prophecy: Ellen G. White and the Women Religious Founders of the Nineteenth Century" (Ph.D. dissertation, Johns Hopkins University, 1983), pp. 196-199.

[50] "John Milton," *World Book Encyclopedia* (1990), vol. 13, p. 556.

[51] 2SG 272.

[52] AA 570.

THE CIVIL WAR VISION
"The Veil"

January 12, 1861

T HE majority of Ellen White's visions were probably recorded fairly soon after the prophet received them. Sometimes, however, there might be a delay of days, weeks, or even months, in the writing out of details. This was the case of the 1890 Salamanca vision in New York, and the 1894 "plowed furrow" vision of an incident on land that later became Avondale College's campus in Australia.

Occasionally the Lord's messenger never did get around to writing out a comprehensive account of a vision at all, in which case we today are dependent upon the records of an eyewitness. A good example of this category would be the first health reform vision, given in the autumn of 1848. It was reported by her husband, James White, some 22 years later, in an article in the November 8, 1870, edition of the *Review and Herald.* [1]

So also with the background and contents of Mrs. White's first vision revealing important information concerning the yet-future U.S. Civil War. That vision was received at Parkville, St. Joseph County, Michigan, on Sabbath, January 12, 1861.

Fortunately, SDA historian J. N. Loughborough was present on the latter occasion. He provides a detailed account in his first book, *Rise and Progress of the Seventh-day Adventists.* Although this work was not published until 1892, we may presume that Loughborough wrote down the incident immediately after it took place. In his preface the author states unequivocally, "Since November 1853 I have kept a diary of daily occurrences. The narrative [in this book] from that date is from the record of this diary." [2]

Parkville is a small village some 30 miles south of Battle Creek,[3] a town so insignificant that today it does not even appear in the *Rand McNally Road Atlas* map of the state of Michigan.[4]

J. N. Andrews and J. N. Loughborough conducted an evangelistic campaign in Parkville in 1859,[5] and as a result raised up a small company. That group is identified in the *Seventh-day Adventist Encyclopedia* as "the first legally organized SDA church," referring to a ceremony that took place on May 13, 1860.[6]

Since the corporate name "Seventh-day Adventist" was not adopted until October 1, four and a half months later,[7] at "one of the most significant SDA gatherings up to that time,"[8] this congregation was obliged to choose its own name. Their "articles of association" reveal that they selected the rather cumbersome title of "Parkville Church of Christ's second advent: taking the Bible as the rule of our faith and discipline"![9]

Doubtless with tongue in cheek, Loughborough, in reporting the event, gently suggested that "perhaps a more appropriate name will be chosen by us as a people; but the church at Parkville concluded to take this name for the present."[10]

A church edifice was constructed subsequently, and an announcement of dedication services, set for January 11 and 12, 1861, duly appeared in the columns of the *Review and Herald*. It invited top church leaders to attend, "and as many more as can come."[11] At the time appointed, an impressive array of church officials appeared to grace the occasion: James and Ellen White, J. H. Waggoner, Uriah Smith, and Loughborough himself.[12] A "large congregation" assembled to hear them and to enjoy the festivities.[13]

Waggoner, who had written three books on SDA doctrine before 1860 (reportedly "with clarity and precision"), and who was also known to be an "eloquent" speaker,[14] was chosen to preach the sermon. James White offered the dedicatory prayer. Ellen followed with "a very powerful exhortation." Moments after she had sat down she was taken off in vision, the duration of which was reported to be "some 20 minutes or more."[15]

A Spiritualist Discomfited

Present in the congregation at Parkville that Sabbath was a Dr. Brown, who was a local physician and a spiritualist. (Such practitioners, which flourished in Mrs. White's day, were generally known either as "electric physicians" or as "magnetic healers.") [16] Dr. Brown had moved to this town in the interim between the close of Loughborough's 1859 evangelistic campaign and the dedication of the church's new edifice on January 12, 1861. [17]

Interestingly, Brown had sent out his own personal invitations to fellow mediums to attend the dedication, when it became known that Mrs. White would attend and speak. His announcement included these words:

"Mrs. White is to be there, and you will hear something good, for she consults with a higher grade of spirits than we do. . . . If Mrs. White comes, she will probably have a vision. If she does, I know just what it is, as a physician; and if she has a vision, I will bring her out of it in a minute." [18]

While Ellen was in vision her husband stepped forward, as he so often did under similar circumstances, and explained the background and nature of his wife's experience. He invited any present who wished to examine her to do so. This not only provided graphic demonstration of the fact that the supernatural was presently at work, but it also served to destroy the credibility of critics who continued to hurl charges of fraud at the Whites.

Witness Loughborough picks up the story at this point: "Just then someone in the back part of the house, where the doctor stood, said, 'Doctor, go ahead and do what you said you would.' We knew not, as yet, what that meant. Brother White, on learning that there was a doctor in the house, invited him to come forward.

"The doctor started in a confident, pompous manner; but when he was about halfway down the aisle, he suddenly stopped, turned deathly pale, and began to shake from head to foot. Brother White urged him to come forward, and he advanced about half of the remaining distance, but stopped in more terror than before.

"Brother White then went to the doctor, put his hand on his shoulder, and urged him forward. The doctor made a careful but hasty examination of the pulse, heart, and breath, and said, 'Elder, her heart and pulse are all right, but there is not any breath in her body.' Of course, he found a different case than he expected.

"When he had finished his examination, he made all haste for the door, trying to get out of the house. Those at the door would not let him out, but said, 'Go back, and do as you said you would.' Brother White, seeing the man trying to get out, said, 'Doctor, please report to the audience the result of your examination.' The doctor said, 'Her heart and pulse are all right, but there is not a particle of breath in the woman's body.'

"The people near the door said, 'Doctor, what is it?' He replied, 'God only knows. Let me out of this house.' They stood back from the door, and he fled. We saw no more of him in our meetings." [19]

Judge Osborne, who was present, then said to Loughborough, "It was evident to all of us that the spirit that controlled the doctor as a medium, and the Spirit that controlled Mrs. White in vision, had no sympathy with each other. The doctor's actions made us think of the evil spirits that wanted to know if the Lord had come to torment them before their time [see Matt. 8:29]." [20]

What the Prophet Saw

What did Mrs. White see in this vision (for she was totally oblivious to the excitement created by Dr. Brown and those who were baiting him during this 20-minute vision)?

After coming out of vision, Mrs. White addressed the congregation, according to eyewitness Loughborough, and said: "There is not a person in this house who has even dreamed of the trouble that is coming upon this land. People are making sport of the secession ordinance of South Carolina, but I have just been shown that a large number of states are going to join that state, and there will be a most terrible war.

"In this vision I have seen large armies of both sides gathered on the field of battle. I heard the booming of the cannon, and saw the dead and dying on every hand. Then I saw them rushing up engaged in hand-to-hand fighting [bayoneting one another].

"Then I saw the field after battle, all covered with the dead and dying. Then I was carried to prisons, and saw the sufferings of those in want, who were wasting away. Then I was taken to the homes of those who had lost husbands, sons, or brothers in the war. I saw there distress and anguish." [21]

Then, surveying her audience, Ellen slowly added a foreboding note: "There are those in this house who will lose sons in that war." [22]

It is important at this point to place this vision and its content in a chronological context:

● December 20, 1860—South Carolina secedes from the Union.

- January 9, 1861—Mississippi secedes.
- January 10, 1861—Florida secedes.
- January 11, 1861—Alabama secedes.
- January 12, 1861—*Ellen White's vision at Parkville, Michigan.*
- January 19, 1861—Georgia secedes.
- January 26, 1861—Louisiana secedes.
- February 1, 1861—Texas secedes.
- February 4, 1861—Constitution of Confederate States of America drafted.
- February 18, 1861—Jefferson Davis inaugurated president of the C.S.A.
- March 4, 1861—Abraham Lincoln inaugurated president of the U.S.A.
- April 12, 1861—C.S.A. military fires on Fort Sumter at Charleston, South Carolina.
- April 15, 1861—Lincoln calls for Union troops to retake Fort Sumter. The C.S.A. regards this act as a declaration of war. Virginia, Arkansas, North Carolina, and Tennessee subsequently join the Confederates.

When Ellen White received her first vision of the U.S. Civil War on January 12, 1861, she, as everyone else in the nation, was aware that South Carolina had seceded from the Union 23 days earlier. However, she may or may not have known of the secession of Mississippi, Florida, and Alabama during the three days immediately preceding her Sabbath vision at Parkville.

It matters little, however, for the firing on Fort Sumter by the Confederate forces—generally considered by American historians as the opening of the Civil War—was still exactly three months future from the day of this vision.

Contemporary Public Opinion

The majority of American historians would probably agree that on the day of her vision the prevailing mood in the North—the "conventional wisdom"—was to the effect that there would most likely be no civil war and if there were, it would be an exceedingly short one, with Union forces winning a quick victory that would summarily end it all.

Illustrative of this attitude (as well as helping to shape it) was Hinton Rowan Helper's 1860 book *The Impending Crisis of the*

South. In a calculated manner it sought to reinforce Northern prejudices that their Southern adversaries were a cloddish, doltish race, with little mechanical aptitude, and virtually incapable of illustrious deeds.

He described a Southern funeral in which the hearse was from the North, the harness on the horses was from the North, the coffin was from the North, as was also the horsewhip in the hands of the driver of the hearse! [23]

Also influential were the published views of Horace Greeley, who editorialized in his New York *Tribune* in late 1860 that it was preposterous for South Carolina to think of separation from the Union.

He told the story of a Scot lad who had made a hole in his neighbor's backyard hedge, the better to slip through and steal fruit from the neighbor's orchard. As the lad began to emerge on the other side, the owner—till now hidden from view—cried out, "Where are you going, sonte?" Whereupon the boy began a retreat as he called out, "Going back again."

The point was clear; but in case the reader missed it, Greeley made the application: All that was necessary was for someone "with the sternness of Jackson" to say, "South Carolina, where are you going?" And they allegedly would quickly reply, "Back again into the Union!" [24]

For good measure, the next week Greeley continued his harangue: "Talk of South Carolina going out of the Union! A few old women with broomsticks could go down there and beat out all of their rebellion!" [25]

Indeed, after war with the North seemed inevitable, Lincoln clearly envisaged a brief campaign. In his appeal mobilizing militia regiments from loyal states to snuff out this "insurrection," he sought only 75,000 troops, and those were called up for only a mere 90 days. [26]

In the face of all this "no war" or "quick war" popular sentiment, Ellen White, three months to the day before war actually broke out, made three predictions: 1. There *would* be war. 2. It would be a *long* war (large armies on both sides, extremely heavy casualties, prisioners of war languishing in enemy camps, etc.). 3. Parents in her immediate audience that day would lose sons in that war.

Predictions Fulfilled

The history of the Civil War is today so well known by Americans that documentation of the fulfillment of her first two points seems superfluous. Concerning the third, Loughborough reports two incidents in which he was personally involved, which are both interesting and germane.

1. Almost exactly one year after the Parkville church dedication, Loughborough returned there for another speaking engagement. Present with him were two men who had heard Ellen White's prediction of a certain, long war, with local SDA families suffering casualties. Their immediate reaction to her words had been total disbelief. Now, a year later, they simply sat there with their heads in their hands sobbing aloud, as Loughborough reminded the congregation of the earlier prediction.

Only six weeks previously one of these men had buried his only son, a victim of the war. The man sitting beside him had lost a son in the war and had a second one facing an extremely doubtful future in a rebel prisoner of war camp. [27]

2. In the autumn of 1883, more than 20 years following Ellen White's prediction of war and tragedy, Loughborough again returned to Parkville, this time to seek out the layman who had served as local elder in 1861 and who was present at the dedication.

"Do you remember her prediction?" he inquired.

"Yes."

"Will you tell me how many you know who were in the house that day who lost sons in the war?"

Whereupon the elder briefly reflected, and then named five families who had so suffered, adding that if he had recourse to his records, which were at home, he thought there might be an additional five families in this category. [28]

In 1891, in preparation for publication of his first history of the SDA Church, Loughborough sought out Martha V. Ensign, then living in Wild Flower, Fresno County, California. From her Loughborough obtained a signed affidavit attesting to the veracity of his account of the prediction and its tragic subsequent fulfillment. Signed on January 30, 1891, the affidavit was published in chapter 21 ("The Civil War in the United States") of the *Rise and Progress of the Seventh-day Adventists.* [29]

As the Civil War progressed, Ellen White was given more visions dealing with that conflict.

Second Civil War Vision

On August 3, 1861, less than eight months after the first Civil War vision, Mrs. White was given an updated view of the conflict while attending a conference of SDA leaders and members at Roosevelt, New York. That date was a day nationally set aside for "humiliation, fasting, and prayer" on behalf of the war effort. In "Slavery and the War," subsequently published in the first volume of *Testimonies for the Church*, she made these particular points:

1. Slavery was a "sin," and laws upholding it were "in direct opposition to the teaching of Christ." [30]

2. God was using the Civil War to punish *both* sides—the South "for [practicing] the sin of slavery"; and the North "for so long suffering its overreaching and overbearing influence." [31]

3. Those who still expected a short war, with the North "to strike a [decisive] blow and end the controversy," would be both surprised and disappointed. [32]

4. Both North and South were deceived concerning each other. Southerners, in reality, "are better prepared for war than has been represented," with "most of their men" being "well skilled in the use of arms, some . . . from experiencing in battle"; in this "they have the advantage of the North." On the other hand, Southerners "have not, as a general thing, the valor and the power of endurance that Northern men have." [33]

5. If the North had taken "active measures" when hostilities first broke out, "this rebellion would have been speedily crushed out." As it had not, however, the South utilized the time to strengthen its position militarily, until "it has become most powerful." [34]

6. Proslavery men and "traitors" in the North, professedly in favor of the union, were extremely influential in government decision-making circles; and some of the actions taken "even favor the South." [35]

7. By far the most amazing revelation in this vision concerned the mysterious and "disastrous battle" at Manassas Junction, Virginia. This battle is known in Union military circles as the "first Battle of Bull Run"; among Confederates it is known as the "First Battle of Manassas." [36] (Many Civil War battles have two names; the Confed-

erates tended to name them after the nearest civilian settlement, while Northerners generally preferred to name them after the nearest body or stream of water!) [37]

An Incredible Revelation

First Bull Run/Manassas was the first major land battle of the Civil War. It was fought near Washington, D.C., in northern Virginia, on July 21, 1861, by armies of nearly equal strength. In vision Ellen White witnessed this "disastrous" battle, characterizing it as "a most exciting, distressing scene." [38]

While both North and South suffered horrendously large casualties, at one point the North was pushing ahead when "an angel descended" from heaven to the battlefield "and waved his hand backward. Instantly there was confusion in the ranks. It appeared to the Northern men that their troops were retreating, when it was not so in reality, and a precipitate retreat commenced. This seemed wonderful [amazing] to me." [39]

Then her angel explained that "God had this nation in His own hand, and would not suffer victories to be gained faster than He ordained." The North was not to be allowed to win a quick, decisive battle, thus ending the war abruptly, because it was to be punished for condoning slavery before the war and also for not making abolition the principal ethical issue in the war. [40]

(At first Lincoln was entirely willing to permit the continuation of slavery, if the Union might thereby be preserved. It was not until January 1, 1863—two years later—that he finally came to the point of making abolition the main stated purpose of the war and issued the Emancipation Proclamation.)

As God "would not permit" an early Northern victory, He "sent an angel to interfere. The sudden falling back of the Northern troops is a mystery to all. They know not that God's hand was in the matter." [41]

Many American Civil War historians recognize a mysterious element in this battle, though understandably, virtually all fail to see a supernatural element in its genesis.

Samuel Eliot Morison and Henry Steele Commager, in their highly respected *Growth of the American Republic, 1000-1865,* characterize this battle as "a scene of extraordinary confusion. For hours it was anyone's battle, although the famous stand of the Stonewall Virginia brigade probably averted a Union victory. Union retreat turned to rout." [42]

Extraordinary *confusion!* This was the very word Ellen White employed in 1861 to describe the scene, after the arrival and interference of the angel!

C.S.A. Lt. Col. W. W. Blackford's personal account of the day's developments supports the account of Ellen White—minus, of course, the descending angel. He had been with "Stonewall" Jackson's forces when, at about 4:00 p.m., "the battle raged with unabated fury. The lines of blue were unbroken and their fire was as vigorous as ever while they surged against the solid walls of gray, standing immovable in their front."

Blackford's attention was momentarily distracted in another direction, when he heard someone shouting, "Look! Look!" He looked back, and "what a change had taken place in an instant. Where those well-dressed, well-defined lines, with clear spaces between, had been steadily pressing forward, the whole field was a confused swarm of men, like bees, running away as fast as their legs could carry them, with all order and organization abandoned. In a moment more the whole valley was filled with them as far as the eye could reach." [43]

Yale University's Ralph H. Gabriel reports tersely, "The Federal assault at first succeeded. The Confederates gave ground and even showed signs of incipient demoralization." But then suddenly, inexplicably, a Southern victory. Gabriel attributes the Confederate success to the brigade of Gen. Thomas Jonathan ("Stonewall") Jackson (who earned his sobriquet that day) as he "stood fast." [44]

Gettysburg College's Gabor S. Boritt [45] and Rice University's Frank E. Van Divier also posit a nonsupernaturalistic explanation, the latter adding a generally accepted assessment that the battle had twofold significance: (1) the North, for the first time, was convinced of the war's seriousness, ending all talk of a "short, quick" war, realizing it faced a long fight ahead; and (2) the Confederate's overconfidence in final victory soared and remained unrealistically high for the next two years, [46] in its own way doubtlessly perpetuating hostilities a bit longer than perhaps otherwise might have been the case.

Third Civil War Vision

On January 4, 1862, some 51 weeks after her first vision on the subject, Ellen White was given her third revelation on the conflict. At this time she was residing in Battle Creek. "I was shown some things in regard to our nation," she soberly reported. They included the following points:

1. Buchanan's administration, which preceded Lincoln's, actually planned and enabled the South to steal Northern weapons of war, so that when hostilities broke out the South would be better prepared than the North! [47]

2. The North did not understand the deep feelings of contempt and hatred the South bore toward them because of its interference in abolition, nor the depth of Southern determination to maintain their "peculiar institution" at all costs. [48]

3. Despite pious mouthings in the North concerning the integrity of the Union, slavery "alone . . . lies at the foundation of the war," [49] in the estimate of Heaven.

4. After one year of war the North was no nearer to victory than when it began (the clear implication being that God would not allow a Northern victory until slavery—not merely the preservation of the Union—was the number one issue). And all accumulated loss of life and property in the war thus far was therefore a tragic waste. [50]

5. Incredibly, proslavery Northern military commanders deliberately exposed antislavery soldiers and officers to hostile fire, and then drew back, so that death would silence their voices and activities! [51]

6. Since the North had not yet made abolition *the* issue, all its official governmental appeals for national fasting by the populace and days of prayer in support of the war effort were—in the eyes of God—"an insult to Jehovah. He accepts no such fasts." [52]

7. Had abolition been the main goal of the North, Great Britain (whose parliament had prohibited the slave trade in 1807, and abolished slavery in the British colonies between 1834 and 1840) [53] would have sided with the Union. Now, however, the British sought their own national interests and were considering siding with the South. [54]

8. Finally, ominously, Ellen White declared, "This nation will yet be humbled into the dust." [55]

Role of Spiritualism

God's angels were not the only ones directly involved in the

American Civil War. Satan and his angels played a major role too. In "The Rebellion," [56] published in early 1863 [57] and based upon an undated vision, Mrs. White reiterated many points made in earlier statements, but this time added an entirely new element: the military were riddled with spiritualism.

"Very many men in authority, generals and officers, act in conformity with instruction communicated by spirits. The spirits of devils, professing to be dead warriors and skillful generals, communicate with men in authority and control many of their movements. One general has directions from these spirits to make special moves and is flattered with the hope of success. Another receives directions which differ widely. . . . Sometimes those who follow the directions given obtain a victory, but more frequently they meet with defeat.

"The spirits sometimes give these leading men an account of events to transpire in battles in which they are about to engage, and of individuals who will fall in the battle. Sometimes it is found to be as these spirits foretold, and this strengthens the faith of the believers in spiritual manifestations. And again it is found that correct information has not been given, but the deceiving spirits make some explanation, which is received. The deception upon minds is so great that many fail to perceive the lying spirits which are leading them on to certain destruction.

"The great leading rebel general, Satan, is acquainted with the transactions of this war, and he directs his angels to assume the form of dead generals, to imitate their manners, and exhibit their peculiar traits of character. And leaders in the army really believe that the spirits of their dead friends and of dead warriors, the fathers of the Revolutionary War, are guiding them." [58]

Again, "Satan has, through his angels, communicated with officers . . . [who have] given up their own judgment and have been led by these lying spirits into very difficult places, where they have been repulsed with dreadful slaughter. It suits his satanic majesty well to see slaughter and carnage upon the earth. He loves to see the poor soldiers mowed down like grass.

"I saw that the rebels have often been in positions where they could have been subdued without much effort; but the communications from the spirits have led the Northern generals and blinded their eyes until the rebels were beyond their reach. And some general would rather allow the rebels to escape than to subdue them.

They think more of the darling institution of slavery than of the prosperity of the nation. These are among the reasons why the war is so protracted." [59]

Conclusion

Hundreds of years before the birth of Christ, the Old Testament prophet Amos had declared that "surely the Lord God will do nothing but he revealeth his secrets unto his servants the prophets" (Amos 3:7). God certainly did reveal many "secrets" concerning the American Civil War to His servant Ellen G. White!

Notes and References

[1] Mrs. White did write in 1851 that tobacco was harmful (letter 5, 1851), and in January 1854 that tea and coffee had been contraindicated by the angel (*Supplement to the Christian Experience and Views of Ellen G. White*, p. 42), but in neither instance were these counsels tied to a specific vision in the autumn of 1848. It remained for her husband to bring everything all together in his more comprehensive statement in the *Review and Herald*, Nov. 8, 1870.

[2] P. iii. This work was revised in 1905, under a new title, *Great Second Advent Movement.*

[3] 1Bio 462.

[4] 1990 ed.

[5] J. N. Loughborough, "Sketches of the Past—No. 122," *Pacific Union Recorder,* Mar. 14, 1912. (Arthur L. White incorrectly dates this evangelistic campaign in the summer of 1860 in 1Bio 462.)

[6] RH, May 29, 1860; SDAE 1044.

[7] RH, Oct. 23, 1860.

[8] SDAE 1044.

[9] RH, May 29, 1860 cf. SDAE 1044.

[10] *Ibid.*

[11] RH, Dec. 18, 1860; cited in 1Bio 462, 263.

[12] William C. White, "Sketches and Memories of James and Ellen White: XXXVIII—The Civil War Crisis," RH, Nov. 26, 1936. (Arthur L. White omits the name of Uriah Smith in his account in 1Bio 463.)

[13] Loughborough, "Sketches of the Past—No. 121," *Pacific Union Recorder,* Mar. 7, 1912.

[14] SDAE 1564.

[15] Loughborough, "Sketches . . . No. 121."

[16] "Shall We Consult Spiritualist Physicians?" RH, June 27, 1882, cited in 5T 198.

[17] Loughborough, "Sketches . . . No. 122."

[18] *Ibid.*

[19] *Ibid.,* pp. 1, 2. (For earlier accounts, cf. RPSDA 97, 98; GCB 1893, p. 60; and GSAM 210, 211.)

[20] *Ibid.,* p. 2.

[21] RPSDA 236, 237; cf. GSAM 338; GCB 1893, p. 60; "Sketches . . . No. 121." Martha D. Amadon, who saw Mrs. White in vision upon a number of occasions, wrote down her recollections on Nov. 24, 1925, at the age of 91 years. She recalls two visions, (a) "the year before the civil war" [1860] and (b) "the last year of the war" [1863]. In the former, Mrs. White spoke in a tent, which would seat about 50, pitched in a pasture by Martha's father, John Byington (in 1863 he would become the first president of the first SDA General Conference). At that meeting Mrs. White is reported to have predicted, "This country will be deluged with blood." The White Estate is unable to confirm the authenticity of this memory statement. The event, if indeed it occurred at all, would have had to take place at least one year earlier than Mrs. Amadon dates it. At her advanced age such confusion as regards dates is quite understandable.

[22] *Ibid.*

[23] Cited in Loughborough, "Sketches . . . No. 121" cf. RPSDA 235, 236.

[24] *Ibid.,* cf. RPSDA 236.

[25] *Ibid.*

[26] "First Battle of Bull Run," *Encyclopedia Americana* (1983), vol. 4, p. 758; "Civil War," *ibid.,* vol. 6, p. 786.

[27] GCB 1893, p. 60.

[28] RPSDA 238, 239.

[29] *Ibid.,* p. 237.

[30] 1T 264.

[31] *Ibid.*

[32] *Ibid.*

[33] *Ibid.,* p. 266.

[34] *Ibid.,* pp. 267, 268.

[35] *Ibid.,* p. 268.

[36] "First Battle of Bull Run," *Encyclopedia Americana.*

[37] "Civil War," *World Book Encyclopedia* (1990), vol. 4, 625.

[38] 1T 266.

[39] *Ibid.,* p. 267.

[40] *Ibid.*

[41] *Ibid.*

[42] New York: Oxford University Press, 1942, pp. 664, 665.

[43] *War Years With Job Stuart* (New York: Scribner and Sons, 1946), pp. 32-35; cited in 2Bio 36-38 (cf. DF956).

[44] "First Battle of Bull Run," *Encyclopedia Americana.*

[45] "Civil War," *World Book Encyclopedia,* pp. 614-635, esp. p. 626.

[46] "U.S. Civil War," *Academic American Encyclopedia* (1983), vol. 5, pp. 15-34; "Battles of Bull Run," *ibid.,* vol. 3, pp. 558, 559.

[47] "The North and the South," 1T 253.

[48] *Ibid.*

[49] *Ibid.,* p. 254.

[50] *Ibid.,* pp. 254, 255.

[51] *Ibid.,* p. 255.

[52] *Ibid.,* p. 257.

[53] *World Book Encyclopedia* (1990), vol. 17, p. 505.

[54] "The North and the South," 1T 258.

[55] *Ibid.,* p. 259.

[56] *Ibid.,* pp. 355-368.

[57] *Ibid.,* p. 716, appendix note to p. 355.

[58] *Ibid.,* pp. 363, 364.

[59] *Ibid.,* pp. 366, 367.

CHAPTER 7

THE HEALTH REFORM VISION
"The Cure"

June 6, 1763

A S noted in chapter 3, all biblical doctrines are true and important, though not all are of equal stature and standing in God's sight. Many doctrines find their proper, rightful place as part of the great "platform" of the truth "as it is in Jesus," while others have been designated as beacon or "pillar" doctrines, primarily serving the function of upholding and supporting the entire platform of truth.

Just so, God had His priorities in the timely introduction of His special health messages to the group that would become known as Seventh-day Adventists. As we survey the topical content of Ellen White's visions during approximately the first 20 years of her ministry, three identifiable categories emerge—one in each of the three successive decades here represented.

This is not to say, however, that only those topics were presented in vision during these periods. Rather, the preeminent emphasis in these decades appears to have focused upon certain particular categories of subjects, for cogent and timely reasons.

God's Three Priorities

1. The first vision was given on an unknown day in December 1844. During the balance of the 1840s—especially during 1848-1850—the predominant emphasis and focus of vision content appear to have been the sorting out and developing of a doctrinal framework of the Seventh-day Adventist belief system of "present truth," as our pioneers were wont to call it.

And not without good reason, for on October 23, 1844, the first day of the Great Disappointment of the Millerites, they had neither message nor audience. It would take no little time of intensive Bible study and reflection before they would have a coherent understanding of (a) the meaning of their disappointment, (b) the three angels' messages of Revelation 14 (especially the third), and (c) a rational justification for a renewed emphasis upon evangelism among unbelievers.

Particularly during 1848-1850 their study tended to crystalize into a somewhat formal structure of doctrinal beliefs, aided and abetted as by a series of "Sabbath Conferences"—six in 1848, six in 1849, and 10 in 1850—held in New York and New England. [1] By December 13, 1850, Ellen White could finally write, "We know that we [now] have the truth." [2]

2. Then God moved to His second priority for the 1850s, the organization of His "remnant" church. Exactly 11 days later, on December 24, 1850, Ellen received her first vision upon this important, necessary subject. Given the substantial impediments that would have to be overcome, it would take a full decade before organization would become a reality.

Finally, in 1860 the first steps in organization were taken: (1) the organization of the "first legally organized" church at Parkville, Michigan, on May 13, [3] (2) the adoption of the corporate name "Seventh-day Adventist," on October 1, [4] and (3) the subsequent organization of the first Seventh-day Adventist institution, the Advent Review Publishing Association, in Battle Creek that same day. [5]

Within the next two years some eight local (state) conferences would be created, culminating in the organization of the General Conference itself on May 21, 1863. [6]

3. With organization now well on its way, the Lord could now turn His attention more directly and fully to His third priority, the development of a health emphasis (quickly to be dubbed the "health message") among Seventh-day Adventists. [7]

Significantly, a mere 16 days after the formal organization of the General Conference, in early June, 1863, Ellen White received her first major health reform vision: "It was at the house of Brother A. Hilliard, at Otsego, Michigan, on June 6, 1863, that the great subject of health reform was opened before me in vision." [8]

Background of the Vision

"Was opened *more fully,*" would perhaps have been the more

accurate expression, for by this time Ellen had already received two
visions dealing, in part, with health-related matters.

In the autumn of 1848 her angel instructed her that tea, coffee,
and tobacco were injurious, even life-threatening.[9] And on February
12, 1854, she was told that (1) adultery was a serious problem in her
church, (2) there was a physically dangerous lack of bodily cleanliness among Sabbathkeepers, and (3) control of appetite was sorely
needed among them.[10]

But now, on Friday, June 5, 1863, there came the first *major*
vision dealing with health concerns. (Although the calendar read
June 5, Ellen dated her vision June 6, since it came after the
beginning of the Sabbath at sunset. She apparently preferred to
emphasize sacred rather than civil time.)[11]

What brought the Whites to Otsego, some 25 miles northwest of
Battle Creek, that memorable weekend? There were at least two
reasons: James White, though still but two months shy of his
forty-second birthday, was suffering signs of what we today would
call "burnout," largely from "constant and excessive labor."[12]
Perhaps the couple both thought a weekend excursion in a rural
setting would tend to revive his flagging spirits. Also, R. J. Lawrence
and M. E. Cornell were conducting an evangelistic tent campaign at
Otsego. "Three or four carriage loads" of people drove up on Friday
as a show of moral support.[13]

Included in the visiting company were George and Martha
Amadon. George, 31, was at this time editor of the *Youth's Instructor*. Martha, 29, who had married George three years earlier, was the
daughter of John Byington, elected two weeks previously as first
president of the General Conference.[14] We are indebted to Martha
for an eyewitness account of what happened next—even if she had to
"peek" during the prayer!

"Friday evening we found ourselves all assembled at Brother
Hilliard's for family worship, about a dozen being present. A chapter
was read and Sister White led in prayer, Brother White kneeling
across the corner from her. Her burden in prayer was for him, and as
she prayed, while still on her knees, she moved over to his side, laid
her hands on his shoulders, and prayed until she was taken in vision.
This lasted for about three quarters of an hour.

"At this time she was given the light on the health reform.
Brother White was also greatly blessed and encouraged, and he was

relieved of the burden of discouragement that he had been carrying." [15]

An initial, partial account of the specific content of this significant vision was written down by Ellen shortly after it was received. About two thirds of the document was counsel given specifically to alleviate James White's deteriorated state of health; the remaining third consisted of general counsels for the church. [16]

In the summer of 1864, however, Ellen White wrote a more complete account of the instruction given her (this time generally omitting personal family counsels). In print it fills some 30 pages, in chapter 39 ("Health"), of *Spiritual Gifts,* book 4. [17] Some 10 categories of counsel are covered in this comprehensive account of this vision.

Ten Categories of Counsel

1. *Care of health is a religious duty.* "I saw that it was a sacred duty to attend to our health, and arouse others to their duty," [18] Ellen wrote. "The body, which God calls His temple, should be preserved in as healthy a condition as possible. Many act as though they had a right to treat their own bodies as they please. They do not realize that God has claims upon them. They are required to glorify Him in their bodies and spirits, which are His. . . . It is a sacred duty which God has enjoined upon reasonable beings, formed in His image, to keep that image in as perfect a state as possible. . . .

"All are required to do what they can to preserve healthy bodies, and sound minds." [19]

She made it clear, however, that man earns nothing toward eternal life, by way of salvation, by following health principles. It is only *after* "man has done all in his power to insure health," by various measures, that "then he is saved alone by a miracle of God's mercy. . . . [Only] then will he be benefited with the atonement of Christ." [20]

2. *The cause of disease is a violation of health laws.* While recognizing that much sickness and disease come from an external invasion of the body by disease-bearing microbes, Ellen still stoutly maintained that much—perhaps most—of disease and illness originated with the "violation of the laws of health," [21] "the laws of their being," [22] "the violation of God's constitution and laws." [23]

She urged her fellow Christians to "reason from cause to

effect," [24] assuring them that God would not work a miracle, either to heal them [25] or yet to preserve their health, [26] if they flouted such laws, even through ignorance.

Much pain and sickness were held, in most cases, to arise from nature's efforts to overcome unnatural conditions resulting from some transgression of nature's laws. [27]

3. *She attacked intemperance on many fronts.* Ellen White lived in an age when the Women's Christian Temperance Union and other similar organizations were most active in publicly attacking intemperance—usually of the alcoholic variety.

Mrs. White was remarkable for her more broad definition of "temperance" ("true temperance teaches us to dispense entirely with everything hurtful and to use judiciously that which is healthful") [28] and her equally broad definition of "intemperance" ("since the Fall [of Adam and Eve], intemperance in almost every form has existed"). [29] For her, intemperance included at least five subcategories:

a. "Stimulating drinks." As might be expected, alcohol came in for attack as a "stimulating drink," an intoxicant that "confused the brain and brought down man to the level of the brute creation." [30] But perhaps much less expected were her equally strong criticisms of tea and coffee. These, she declared, "are stimulating. Their effects are similar to those of tobacco; but they affect in a less degree." [31]

Mrs. White recognized the dangers of addiction to these substances, pointing out that when efforts were made to break from these "slow poisons," symptoms of "dizziness, headache, numbness, nervousness, and irritability" would appear. But if the victims were "determined in their efforts to persevere and overcome, abused nature will soon again rally, and perform her work wisely and well without these stimulants." [32]

b. Tobacco, "in whatever form," is a "slow and sure" poison [33] (including snuff). [34] "It affects the brain and benumbs the sensibilities, so that the mind cannot clearly discern spiritual things, especially those truths which would have a tendency to correct this filthy indulgence. Those who use tobacco in any form are not clear before God." [35]

Later in the chapter she added, significantly, "Tobacco is a poison of the most deceitful and malignant kind, having an exciting, then a paralyzing influence upon the nerves of the body. It is all the more dangerous because its effects upon the system are so slow, and at first scarcely perceivable. . . . Multitudes have surely murdered themselves by this slow poison." [36]

Please note her three adjectives: "slow," "deceitful," and "malignant." (By 1886 she would slightly revise her characterization to read "slow, insidious, but most malignant poison.") [37]

c. Highly spiced foods came under the rubric of intemperance, specifically, "highly seasoned [flesh] meats" and "rich gravies"; [38] "rich cake, pies, and puddings"; [39] and "various kinds of rich . . . preserves." [40] Such "rich food breaks down the healthy organs of body and mind"; causes children, in particular, to become "feeble, pale, and dwarfed." Such "spices" are to be eschewed because they "have a tendency to excite the animal passions." [41]

d. Overwork. "Intemperance in labor" [42] had a special application to Ellen's husband, James, who was a chronic "workaholic." [43] But also singled out in particular were housewives whose slavery to a hot cookstove resulted in the neglect of their children, ill temper, and a beclouding of the reasoning faculties, with consequent fading of spirituality. [44] Habits of working, Ellen was assured, had a very definite effect upon one's health. [45]

e. "Indulgence of base passions," not otherwise more specifically identified, was an obvious reference to intemperate sexual relationships. These were reported to have a tendency to benumb "the fine sensibilities, so that sacred things have been placed upon a level with common things." [46] "Corrupt" and "debasing passions," given "loose rein," in "great measure" destroy the "reasoning faculties." [47] God was now calling for "purity of heart." [48]

4. *Vegetarianism* was, for the first time, revealed to Ellen as the ideal diet, being the original diet of Adam and Eve in Eden before death became a factor in human existence. [49] Now, a "wholesome diet," consisting of fruits, vegetables, and "plain" (whole-grain) bread, was the ideal. [50]

Recognizing that God had permitted "clean" animals (as later defined by Leviticus 11) to be eaten after the Noachian flood, animal food was nevertheless "not the most healthy article of food for man"; [51] it was a chief factor in dramatically shortening the life of the postdiluvians.

Later, during the Exodus, although God did not prohibit Israel from eating a flesh diet altogether He withheld it from them "in great measure," [52] providing instead the daily manna. As for today, "many die of diseases caused wholly by meat-eating, yet the world does not seem to be the wiser." [53]

Pork, however, was totally prohibited to ancient literal Israel, and Ellen White made the extension to modern, "spiritual" Israel. Five years earlier, in 1858, she had rebuked the Stephen N. Haskells ("Brother and Sister A") for making the eating of pork a test of church membership. [54] Now she was shown that from ingesting swine's flesh the human body would suffer from "scrofula, leprosy, and cancerous humors," [55] for "pork-eating is still causing the most intense suffering to the human race." [56]

5. Proper dietary habits now called for the control of appetite, which had "been indulged to the injury of health." [57] The twin habits of too-frequent eating between regular meals and eating too much ("gluttony") [58] had an ill effect upon the stomach, which needs regular periods of rest. A two-meal-a-day dietary program was highly preferred; the third, an evening meal, if taken at all, should be "light," and be eaten several hours before bedtime. [59]

6. *Control of the mind* was an essential feature of this vision. Mrs. White wrote: "There is a class of invalids who have no real located disease. But as they believe they are dangerously diseased, they are in reality invalids. The mind is diseased, and many die who might recover of disease, which exists alone in the imagination."

Again: "The power of the will is a mighty soother of the nerves, and can resist much disease, simply by not yielding to ailments, and settling down into a state of inactivity. Those who have but little force, and natural energy, need to constantly guard themselves, lest their minds become diseased, and they give up to supposed disease, when none really exists." [60]

7. *Natural remedies in healing.* Mrs. White inveighed heavily against the contemporary practice of physicians in her day in prescribing "poisonous," "powerful" drugs and "dangerous mixtures," [61] such as *nux vomica* (strychnine), opium, mercury, calomel, and quinine. [62]

"Nature alone is the effectual restorer." "Nature alone possesses curative powers." [63]

The "natural" remedies focused upon in this first major health reform vision were: (a) pure air, [64] (b) pure water—both for internal and external needs, [65] (c) sunshine, [66] (d) physical exercise, [67] (e) adequate rest, [68] and (f) fasting for brief periods to give the stomach rest. [69]

(While only hinted at inferentially in this vision, "a firm trust in God," or "trust in divine power" was added 22 years later, in 1885, to round out Ellen's final, complete list of natural remedies.) [70]

8. The subject of *personal cleanliness* had been raised in the 1854 vision at Brookfield, New York, as noted above; now it was reemphasized and broadened to include the body, clothing, and living quarters. [71] God had "required the children of Israel to observe habits of strict cleanliness." He was "still a God of cleanliness," and personal cleanliness was now placed on the level of "purity of heart" as an obligation of all professing Christians. [72]

9. *Environmental concerns* were included in this vision, with counsel to remove decaying vegetation (and even shade trees and shrubbery) from too-close proximity to family dwellings, to prevent occupants from breathing in the "effluvia" that such tended to generate. Wherever possible, houses should be built upon high, dry ground, because lowland locations tended to foster the settling of water, which in turn would produce a "poisonous miasma" that caused fever, ague, sore throat, lung diseases, and fever. [73]

10. *Health education* by the church, with particular reference to prevention of illness, rounded out the multifaceted counsel of the 1863 health reform vision. "I saw that it was a sacred duty to attend to our health, and arouse others to their duty. . . . We have a duty to speak, to come out against intemperance of every kind. . . . I saw that we should not be silent upon the subject of health, but should wake up minds to the subject.

"I saw that our children should be instructed, and we should take time to teach them." [74]

Contemporary Attitudes Toward Health

None of the above sounds very unusual to us today, until we take into account the attitudes toward health that prevailed in the mid-nineteenth century, when Ellen White first wrote upon the subject.

Radio-TV commentator Paul Harvey, in a nationally syndicated United Features column, aptly characterized the age as "an era of medical ignorance bordering on barbarism," when "doctors were still bloodletting and performing surgery with unwashed hands." [75]

In 1974 Otto L. Bettmann, founder of the internationally famous archive in New York that bears his name, wrote an exceedingly fascinating book about conditions in the "Gay Nineties." He entitled it *The Good Old Days—They Were Terrible!* Illustrated with photographs and line-drawing engravings of the period, the book gives a graphic look into this now-bygone day. [76]

Of particular interest in the context of the 1863 health reform vision are his chapters dealing with air, housing, food and drink, and health.

In 1890 Dr. John Harvey Kellogg wrote the preface to *Christian Temperance and Bible Hygiene* (the only book ever to be written jointly by James and Ellen White). In it the doctor offered "a few facts of interest" to readers:

"1. At the time [these] writings . . . first appeared, the subject of health was almost wholly ignored, not only by the people to whom they were addressed, but by the world at large.

"2. The few advocating the necessity of a reform in physical habits propagated in connection with the advocacy of genuine reformatory principles the most patent and in some instances disgusting errors.

"3. Nowhere, and by no one, was there presented a systematic and harmonious body of hygienic truths, free from patent errors, and consistent with the Bible and the principles of the Christian religion."

Several paragraphs later the good doctor returned to his main point:

"It must certainly be regarded as a thing remarkable, and evincing unmistakable evidence of divine insight and direction, that in the midst of confused and conflicting teachings, claiming the authority of science and experience, but warped by ultra notions and rendered impotent for good by the great admixture of error—it must be admitted to be something extraordinary that a person making no claims to scientific knowledge or erudition should have been able to organize, from the confused and error-tainted mass of ideas advanced by a few writers and thinkers on health subjects, a body of hygienic principles so harmonious, so consistent, and so genuine that the discussions, the researches, the discoveries, and the experience of a quarter of a century have not resulted in the overthrow of a single principle, but have only served to establish the doctrines taught." [77]

Seven years after he had penned these words, Dr. Kellogg

addressed a General Conference in session, on March 3, 1897, upon the same subject. He added: "Every single statement with reference to healthful living, and the general principles that underlie the subject, have been verified by scientific discovery. . . . There is not a single principle in relation to the healthful development of our bodies and minds that is advocated in these writings from Sister White, which I am not prepared to demonstrate conclusively from scientific evidence. . . . The writings 30 years ago are fully substantiated by the scientific discoveries of today." [78]

Even more remarkable, then, is the personal testimony of the late Dr. Clive M. McCay, who spent his entire 35-year teaching career (1927-1962) at Cornell University. He authored or coauthored more than 150 scientific papers on various aspects of nutrition. One of his areas of expertise was the history of nutrition.

Dr. McCay's contribution to that science was so significant that upon his death in 1967 the *Journal of the American Dietetic Association* published a comprehensive life sketch, [79] and the *Journal of Nutrition* devoted 10 full pages to a retrospective survey of his life and work. [80]

Dr. McCay refused to date the beginning of modern nutritional science earlier than 1900 (by which time Ellen White had penned perhaps the majority of her writings on health and diet). Nearly all writings on nutrition before 1900 consisted mainly of arrant nonsense; yet, said Dr. McCay in a three-part series of articles written for the *Review and Herald* in 1959, Mrs. White's "basic concepts about the relation between diet and health have been verified to an unusual degree by scientific advances of the past decades. Someone may attempt to explain this remarkable fact by saying: 'Mrs. White simply borrowed her ideas from others.' But how would she know which ideas to borrow and which to reject out of the bewildering array of theories and health teachings current in the nineteenth century? She would have had to be a most amazing person, with knowledge beyond her times, in order to do this successfully!"

Dr. McCay concluded authoritatively, "In spite of the fact that the works of Mrs. White were written long before the advent of modern scientific nutrition, no better overall guide is available today." [81]

A Unique Contribution

While Mrs. White's views have been further corroborated to an amazing degree by scientific research conducted as recently as the decade of the 1980s, which because of limited space must remain undocumented here, [82] it was perhaps in her concept of linking man's physical condition with his religious experience that Mrs. White made her most unique contribution.

Virtually none of the Christian bodies in the 1860s felt that physical health had anything to do with Christian theology. Had any minister presumed to raise the issue in the pulpit, he would quickly have been put in his place.

Yet Ellen White clearly linked the two: "The health of the body is to be regarded as essential for growth in grace and the acquirement of an even temper," [83] she told the delegates to the 1909 General Conference session.

As early as 1866 J. H. Waggoner recognized the uniqueness of this concept. He wrote in the pages of the *Review and Herald:* "We do not profess to be pioneers in the general principles of the health reform. The facts on which this movement is based have been elaborated, in a great measure, by reformers, physicians, and writers on physiology and hygiene, and so may be found scattered through the land. But we do claim that by the method of God's choice it has been more clearly and powerfully unfolded, and is thereby producing an effect which we could not have looked for from any other means.

"As mere physiological and hygienic truths, they might be studied by some at their leisure, and by others laid aside as of little consequence; but when placed on a level with the great truths of the third angel's message by the sanction and authority of God's Spirit, and so declared to be the means whereby a weak people may be made strong to overcome, and our diseased bodies cleansed and fitted for translation, then it comes to us as an essential part of *present truth,* to be received with the blessing of God, or rejected at our peril." [84]

The uniqueness still obtained 107 years after Waggoner wrote those lines. In 1973 psychiatrist Karl Menninger, in his perceptive seminal work, *Whatever Became of Sin?* singled out Seventh-day Adventists, together with the Latter-day Saints and the followers of Islam, as being virtually the only major exponents of the view that "the taking of coffee and tea and tobacco [is] harmful and hence *sinful."* [85]

Scientific Corroboration

Science has confirmed virtually all the counsels that emanated from Ellen White's first major health reform vision of 1863. Limitations of space prevent mention here of more than perhaps four points made that found their corroboration in scientific inquiry between 1950 and 1990:

1. *Tobacco.* In 1863 Ellen White declared that tobacco was a "slow," "deceitful" (in 1886 this adjective was modified to read "insidious"), and "malignant" (in 1886, "most malignant") poison. Has history subsequently borne this out?

In the early 1950s Alton Oschner, M.D., professor of thoracic surgery at Tulane University's medical school, New Orleans, was among the earliest to demonstrate an undeniable link between cigarette smoking and lung cancer.[86] And the three characterizations by Ellen White?

a. "Slow": Medical pathologists today declare that it takes approximately 20 years to incubate a full-blown case of lung cancer.

b. "Deceitful" or "insidious": Medical specialists also tell us that if the patients wait for the overt symptoms of lung cancer to appear, it is usually too late to save their lives. The patients with this disease who *are* saved are those whose condition is revealed in the early stages as a result of routine X-rays.

c. "Most malignant": No informed medical scientist today would dispute the demonstrated link between cigarette smoking and lung cancer.

Ellen White was about 90 years ahead of her time on this one!

2. *Coffee.* Ellen White was told by an angel from heaven in the autumn of 1848, and again in the spring of 1863, that the drinking of coffee was deleterious to health, even life-threatening.

In the March 12, 1981, *New England Journal of Medicine* veteran epidemiologist Dr. Brian MacMahon reported on a study done by his team of Harvard University School of Public Health researchers. According to their study, the predisposing cause of cancer of the pancreas (one of the fastest killers of all cancers today) is coffee drinking.

Then he "dropped the other shoe" by adding that caffeine was probably not the chief culprit, since in his study group as many patients died from drinking decaffeinated coffee as those who died using the straight stuff. [87]

Unsurprisingly, the coffee industry lobbyists quickly geared for a frontal attack on the study and its presenters; indeed, their livelihood and the survival of their industry depended upon destroying the substantial impact this report (in one of the nation's most respected medical journals) had created.

A five-page article, "All About Caffeine," by Lowell Ponte, appeared in the January 1983 *Reader's Digest* in what was billed as "A Reader's Digest Report to Consumers." It tried to destroy the credibility of the MacMahon report. [88]

Mervyn G. Hardinge, M.D., Ph.D., Dr.P.H., then director of the Health/Temperance Department of the General Conference of Seventh-day Adventists, responded in these words:

"This article is obviously written by one who is defensive of the use of caffeine. After some 25-30 years of countless articles showing that tobacco smoke is detrimental to health, scientists who smoke still claim there is no hard evidence to relate smoking to human illness in the smoker.

"The same is and will be true of those who use caffeine. I know of no way to discount an article like this because no matter how carefully a study is put together, someone can criticize its structure, methodology, interpretation, etc. I think our best course is to, whenever possible, present the evidence as we see it and allow the individual to choose his own course.

"I think caffeine is addictive (I am a pharmacologist), increases the incidence of coronary heart disease, is an adjunct to hypertension and consequential stroke, is a real instigator of peptic and duodenal ulcers, produces birth defects (has long been known to affect chromosomes), and in recent reports coming from the Adventist Health Study, is related to a significant increase in cancer. I doubt, however, if the *Reader's Digest* would be willing to print such an article." [89]

3. *Vegetarianism.* Ellen White first learned of the substantial health hazards of a nonvegetarian diet in 1863; she herself became a vegetarian immediately thereafter. [90] In 1900 she wrote: "Animals are becoming more and more diseased, and it will not be long until animal food will be discarded by many besides Seventh-day Adventists." [91]

Perhaps the most recent distinguished non-Adventist scientist to come forward urging vegetarianism is Dean Ornish, M.D. His professional pedigree is impressive: assistant clinical professor of medicine, University of California, San Francisco, School of Medicine; attending physician, Pacific Presbyterian Medical Center, San Francisco; and president and director, Preventive Medicine Research Institute, Sausalito, California.

His recent findings were little short of startling. Writing in *Hospital Practice,* May 15, 1991 ("Can Lifestyle Change Reverse Coronary Atherosclerosis?"), Ornish reported that "by combining a strict low-fat vegetarian diet, moderate aerobic exercise, abstinence from smoking, and stress management training" his study group was able to show "measurable regression of disease in patients with severe coronary atherosclerosis." [92]

Recently challenged on his view, Ornish ticked off the reasons for his vegetarian stance:

• "Even severely blocked arteries began to unclog in the majority of heart patients when they stopped eating animal products and made other simple lifestyle changes." Atherosclerosis can be reversed!

• A December 13, 1990, study in the *New England Journal of Medicine* provides persuasive new evidence that the more red meat and animal fat women ate, the more likely they were to get colon cancer. Harvard's Dr. Walter Willett, chief director of the study, declared, "The optimum amount of red meat you should eat should be zero."

• Dr. T. Colin Campbell, of Cornell University, directed a landmark study of 6,500 persons in mid-1990. He found that "the more meat they ate, the more likely they were to die prematurely from coronary heart disease, colon cancer, breast cancer, prostate cancer, and lung cancer, among others."

• "Many athletes are forgoing the pregame steak for foods high in complex carbohydrates because they find that eating less meat often increases their endurance."

• Most beef is "still very high in fat. And cholesterol. Studies also indicate that meat protein and perhaps other substances in beef raise the risk of cancer and heart disease."

• "Eating meat makes you fat."

In his conclusion Dr. Ornish played on a recent slogan of the

American Beef Association ("Beef. Real food for real people.") with the words "Meat. Real food for real death." [93]

4. *Trust in Divine Power.* Ellen White listed this as one of "nature's remedies." Although I firmly believe it, I never expected to find an empirical study demonstrating the veracity of her declaration. But now science has confirmed the value of even this "natural remedy"! The respected *Southern Medical Journal* of July 1988, included an article by Randolph C. Bird entitled the "Positive Therapeutic Effects of Intercessory Prayer in a Coronary Care Unit Population." [94] The two questions his study sought to answer were: (1) "Does intercessory prayer to the Judeo-Christian God have any effect on the patient's medical condition and recovery?" and (2) "How are these effects characterized, if present?"

His study concludes with these findings: "Prayers to the Judeo-Christian God were made on behalf of the patients in the prayer [study] group by 'born again' believers in Jesus Christ. Analysis of events after entry into the study showed the prayer group had less congestive heart failure, required less diuretic and antibiotic therapy, had fewer episodes of pneumonia, had fewer cardiac arrests, and were less frequently intubated and ventilated. . . .

"In this study I have attempted to determine whether intercessory prayer to the Judeo-Christian God has any effect on the medical condition and recovery of hospital patients. I have further attempted to measure any effects, if present, of those prayers. Based on these data there seemed to be an effect, and that effect was presumed to be beneficial." [95]

Conclusion

Norman M. Kaplan, M.D., professor of internal medicine and head of the hypertension section of the University of Texas' Southwestern Medical School at Dallas, is considered one of the foremost (if not the number one) authority on hypertension (high blood pressure) in the world. Speaking to more than 1,000 health-care professionals attending the Lifestyle Medicine convention at Loma Linda University School of Health in the summer of 1983, Dr. Kaplan addressed particularly the Seventh-day Adventists in his audience with these words:

"You as Adventists may have espoused a certain dietary lifestyle on the basis of faith, in the past; but now you can practice it on the basis of scientific evidence. Hopefully you will not [go back and re] join the main stream, but [rather] adhere to your health heritage." [96]

One year later William Herbert Foege, M.D., M.P.H., director for the Center for Disease Control, United States Public Health Service, Atlanta, Georgia, under the administrations of Presidents Jimmy Carter and Ronald Reagan (1977-1983), spoke at a Loma Linda University School of Health "Update" on Monday, March 5, 1984. He declared emphatically, "You Seventh-day Adventists are now the role model for the rest of the world." [97]

Notes and References

[1] "Sabbath Conferences," SDAE 1255, 1256.

[2] Letter 30, 1850; cited in 1Bio 194.

[3] RH, May 29, 1860; SDAE 1044.

[4] RH, Oct. 23, 1860.

[5] SDAE 1212.

[6] *Ibid.*, p. 493.

[7] Dores Eugene Robinson, *The Story of Our Health Message* (Nashville: Southern Pub. Assn. 1955), 3rd ed., p. 75.

[8] RH, Oct. 8, 1867.

[9] James White, in RH, Nov. 8, 1870; cf. Robinson, pp. 65-70.

[10] 3SM 273-275.

[11] 3Index 2980, note on vision of June 6.

[12] 1T 517.

[13] W. C. White, "Sketches and Memories of James and Ellen White—XXXVII: Light on Healthful Living," RH, Nov. 12, 1936.

[14] SDAE 36.

[15] Martha D. Amadon, "Mrs. E. G. White in Vision," *Notebook Leaflets From the Elmshaven Library*, DF 105c.

[16] At the time Robinson wrote his work the document was designated as letter 4, 1863; it has since been reclassified as Ms 1, 1863, p. 6; cited in Robinson, p. 77.

[17] 4aSG 148.

[18] MS 1, 1863, p. 6, cited in Robinson, p. 77.

[19] 4aSG 148.

[20] *Ibid.*, pp. 148, 149.

[21] *Ibid.*, pp. 120, 134.

[22] *Ibid.*, p. 137.

[23] *Ibid.*, p. 124.

[24] *Ibid.*, p. 137.

[25] *Ibid.*, pp. 148, 149.

[26] *Ibid.*, pp. 144, 145.

[27] W. C. White, "Sketches and Memories."

[28] PP 562.

[29] 4aSG 120.

[30] *Ibid.*, p. 125.

[31] *Ibid.*, p. 128.

[32] *Ibid.*, pp. 128, 129.

[33] *Ibid.*, p. 126.

[34] *Ibid.*, p. 129.

[35] *Ibid.*, p. 126.

[36] *Ibid.*, p. 128.

[37] MS, 29, 1886, pp. 1-4; cited in 3MR 115 and SD 212.

[38] 4aSG 129.

[39] *Ibid.*, p. 130.
[40] *Ibid.*
[41] *Ibid.*, p. 132.
[42] *Ibid.*, p. 131.
[43] MS 1, 1863, pp. 2-5.
[44] 4aSG 132.
[45] *Ibid.*, p. 134.
[46] *Ibid.*, p. 124.
[47] *Ibid.*, p. 131.
[48] *Ibid.*, p. 128.
[49] *Ibid.*, p. 120.
[50] *Ibid.*, pp. 130, 132.
[51] *Ibid.*, pp. 120, 121.
[52] *Ibid.*, pp. 121, 122.
[53] *Ibid.*, p. 147.
[54] 1T 206, 207.
[55] 4aSG 146.
[56] *Ibid.*
[57] *Ibid.*, p. 124.
[58] *Ibid.*, p. 130.
[59] *Ibid.*, pp. 129, 130, 133.
[60] *Ibid.*, pp. 145, 146.
[61] *Ibid.*, pp. 134, 135, 137, 139.
[62] *Ibid.*, pp. 138, 139.
[63] *Ibid.*, pp. 134, 136.
[64] *Ibid.*, pp. 133, 138, 142, 143.
[65] *Ibid.*, pp. 133-137, 141, 143.
[66] *Ibid.*, pp. 142, 143.
[67] *Ibid.*, pp. 145, 146.
[68] *Ibid.*, p. 146.
[69] *Ibid.*, p. 133.
[70] 5T 443; MH 127.
[71] 4aSG 140, 141.
[72] *Ibid.*, pp. 126-128.
[73] *Ibid.*, pp. 141, 144.
[74] MS 1, 1863, p. 6.
[75] *Today's Health,* Winter 1960, back page.
[76] New York: Random House, 1974.
[77] Battle Creek, Mich.: Good Health Pub. Co., 1890, pp. iii, iv.
[78] GCB 1897, pp. 309, 310.
[79] *Journal of the American Dietetic Association* 53 (July 1968): 69.
[80] *Journal of Nutrition* 103 (January 1973): 1-10.
[81] RH, Feb. 26, 1959; cited in Francis D. Nichol, *Why I Believe in Mrs. E. G. White* (Washington, D.C.: Review and Herald Pub. Assn., 1964), pp. 58, 59.
[82] See Roger W. Coon, "E. G. White, M.D.? Current Research Evaluates Her Counsels on Health," *Dialogue* 3, No. 1: 11-13, 28, 29.
[83] 9T 160. For a more extensive exposition of the crucial significance of the relation of the brain to Christianity, see the new compilation, *Counsels for the Church* (1989), which condenses the nine-volume *Testimonies* series in one book, chapter 16 (pp. 117-123). The very first three statements are taken, respectively, from 2T 347; 3T 50, 51; and Te 13, 14.
[84] RH, Aug. 7, 1866; cited in Robinson, pp. 79, 80.
[85] New York: Hawthorn Books, Inc., 1973, p. 142. (Italics supplied.)
[86] Oschner's cinema film (in which he appeared personally), *One in 20,000,* produced in 1954, took its title from the fact that in that year, just in the U.S.A., 20,000 lung cancer patients died of this disease. The film was produced and distributed by the Temperance Department of the General Conference of the SDA Church (interview with Winton Beaven, Ph.D., Kettering, Ohio, July 8, 1991). Some 30 years after *One in 20,000* was released, the annual American death toll from lung cancer reached 121,000 (of a total of 139,000 cases), a more than 600 percent increase in three decades. Women did not begin to smoke in large numbers

until the early 1940s, so female fatalities from lung cancer began to loom large in the early 1960s. By February of 1984 lung cancer surpassed breast cancer as the leading *cancer* cause of American women fatalities from disease. By October 1986 lung cancer was the leading cause of death among American women from *all* causes.

[87] Brian MacMahon, Stella Yen, Dimitrius Trichpoulos, Kenneth Warren, and George Nardi, "Coffee and Cancer of the Pancreas," *New England Journal of Medicine* 304, No. 11 (Mar. 12, 1981): 630-633. Reports were also carried in *Newsweek*, Mar. 23, 1981, p. 87, and *Time*, Mar. 23, 1981, p. 73.

[88] PP 72-76.

[89] Mervyn G. Hardinge to Roger W. Coon, Washington, D.C., Jan. 11, 1983.

[90] CD 482-484.

[91] 7T 124.

[92] P. 107. This article covers pp. 107-114.

[93] "For a Better Life, Don't Eat Any Beef," *USA Today,* International Edition, Dec. 19, 1990, p. 5-A.

[94] PP 826-829.

[95] *Ibid.,* p. 829.

[96] Cited in *Far Eastern Division Outlook,* August 1983, p. 12.

[97] At the time of Dr. Foege's Loma Linda address he held the post of assistant U.S. surgeon general and special assistant for policy development in the U.S. Department of Health and Human Services. Since the summer of 1986 he has served jointly as executive director and Fellow for International and Domestic Health of the Carter Center of Emory University, a consortium of nonprofit organizations that "seek to alleviate conflict, reduce suffering, and promote better understanding among peoples" of the world (D. Louise Coon to Roger W. Coon, Carter Center, Atlanta, Georgia, June 12, 1991).

For Further Reading:

Foster, Vernon W., M.D. *New Start!* 3rd ed. Santa Barbara, Calif.: Woodbridge Press, 1989. 269 pp.

Reid, George W. *A Sound of Trumpets: Americans, Adventists, and Health Reform.* Washington, D.C.: Review and Herald Pub. Assn., 1982. 190 pp.

Schoepflin, Rennie B. "Health and Health Care," in Gary Land, ed. *The World of Ellen G. White.* Washington, D.C.: Review and Herald Pub. Assn., 1987. Pp. 143-160.

Van Dolson, Leo. *The Golden Eight: Eight Dynamic Golden Rules That Lead to Total Health.* Washington, D.C.: Review and Herald Pub. Assn., 1977. 95 pp.

White, Ellen G. *Adventures in Adventist Living: A Call to Better Living Evangelism.* Boston: SDA Community Services Van Ministry, 1987. 61 pp.

THE NATHANIEL DAVIS VISION
"The Exorcism"

August 16, 1897

THE late H.M.S. Richards, founder of the Voice of Prophecy radiobroadcast ministry, visited the West African metropolis of Ibadan, Nigeria, in August 1953. He held a meeting for students and graduates of his Bible correspondence school, and also for the general public. His audience consisted of animists, Muslims, a sprinkling of Christians of various persuasions, and persons of no religion whatever. Some probably had never even heard the name of Jesus.

The radio evangelist preached a heart-touching sermon, "The Three Great Circles of God's Love." The largest of these concentric circles, he said, was revealed in John 3:16: "God so loved the *world* . . ." The second: "Christ also loved the *church*" (Eph. 5:25). The third and smallest circle of God's love: Jesus "loved *me*, and gave himself for *me*" (Gal. 2:20).

A favorite and frequent theme of Ellen White's was God's love, concern, and care for the individual sinner. She introduced her commentary on the lost sheep by pointing out that in Christ's well-known parable, "the shepherd goes out to search for one sheep—the very least that can be numbered. So if there had been but one lost soul, Christ would have died for that one." [1]

In that same context, but in another book, she expands the theme: "Jesus knows us individually, and is touched with the feeling of our infirmities. He knows us all by name. He knows the very house in which we live, the name of each occupant. He has at times given directions to His servants to go to a certain street in a certain city, to such a house, to find one of His sheep.

"Every soul is as fully known to Jesus as if he were the only one for whom the Saviour died. The distress of every one touches His heart. The cry for aid reaches His ear. He came to draw all men unto Himself. . . . He cares for each one as if there were not another on the face of the earth." [2]

Lest her reader feel that the great Sovereign Superintendent of the universe is so preoccupied with cosmic, intergalactic concerns that He cannot notice one insignificant, struggling soul upon Planet Earth, Mrs. White urges with a ring of triumph:

"Keep your wants, your joys, your sorrows, your cares, and your fears before God. You cannot burden Him; you cannot weary Him. He who numbers the hairs of your head is not indifferent to the wants of His children. . . . His heart of love is touched by our sorrows and even by our utterances of them. Take to Him everything that perplexes the mind. Nothing is too great for Him to bear, for He holds up worlds, He rules over all the affairs of the universe. Nothing that in any way concerns our peace is too small for Him to notice." [3]

Not surprisingly, Satan too "cares" for the individual, as Mrs. White also noted. Taking off from a popular nineteenth-century motif of the "game of life," she spoke of the devil finding "satisfaction" [4] as he plays the game of life for every soul. [5]

Furthermore, "if Satan sees that he is in danger of losing one soul, he will exert himself to the utmost to keep that one. And when the individual is aroused to his danger, and, with distress and fervor, looks to Jesus for strength, Satan fears that he will lose a captive, and he calls a reinforcement of his angels to hedge in the poor soul, and form a wall of darkness around him, that heaven's light may not reach him." [6]

This being the case, it is not surprising that many of the visions and prophetic dreams of the prophets, from biblical times to modern, focused upon the struggles and salvation of one single person. Such was the case with Nathaniel Davis of Australia.

A Recent Convert

Nathaniel A. Davis was a convert to Seventh-day Adventism probably sometime near the midpoint of Ellen White's nine-year missionary career "down under" (1891-1900).

Davis, described by one minister who knew him well as a tall, lanky man "of about six feet five inches," [7] was for a time connected with the Bible Echo publishing enterprise. He had served variously as a colporteur (gospel literature salesperson) and a circulator of religious liberty petitions. Ellen White subsequently characterized him as a man with "advantages in education, . . . pleasing abilities," with "clear insight into [God's] word," and "blessed . . . with powers to communicate that word in an acceptable manner." [8]

Our first glimpse of "Nattie" Davis (as his friends called him) in the archives of the Ellen G. White Estate comes from a lengthy eight-page handwritten letter he wrote to Ellen White on September 9, 1896, from Brisbane. In great agony of soul he introduces himself by confessing:

"I have dishonored my Lord, disgraced my profession, made shipwreck of faith, and am now in despair, for I see only the blankest ruin and the direst need confronting me and have no one to blame but myself." [9]

Describing his emotional state tersely, he added: "I cannot pray; it chokes me to attempt to sing. I am a living lie, and I am ready to sink into utter despair. Yet in spite of all and base as I am, I love the truth, I love the Saviour, I desire to do right, God knows I do; and yet I wonder myself how I can, for my life is full of wrongdoings and contemptible motives."

"I am willing to do anything the Lord may direct, to follow in any course He may open up. But He seems not to hear me and I dread His wrath. Pray for me; beseech a testimony from the Lord regarding my case. I will submit to His word; only direct me, and I will follow." [10]

He closed his letter with the self-description: "Yours in fear and trembling." [11]

Davis' immediate problems revolved around a tragic sequence of debt incurred from default against borrowed money, which, in turn, had been prompted, he said, by "personal enmities, greed, and envy." It resulted in his losing his position as colporteur.

Owing large sums to both customers and the publishing house, stranded in Brisbane, and "backslidden," as he himself characterized his present state, he was unable to find secular employment because of the Sabbath. "I am . . . helpless to do anything. I am ashamed to beg and dare not steal. . . . I am in terror lest my wife should discover how things are," and desert. [12]

Mrs. White seems not to have responded immediately—perhaps

the "testimony from the Lord" regarding Davis's case had not yet been given. So three months later, on December 18, 1896, Davis again took pen in hand to plead for help:

"I know well that you are very busy and perhaps I ought not to have expected that you should have spent any time or trouble over me. Yet I plead for the voice of counsel. I have the most unbounded confidence in your gift and am sure that the Lord would listen to your prayer and give me some light on the dark path that seems now to lie before me."

The noose of debt seemed ever more tightly constricting his neck, he declared. "I lose heart. Surely the Lord has cast me off. I feel a sense of despair. It seems as though I were guilty of all the sins of the world. The lake of fire yawns before me. I can never get ready in time. I fear lest I should perish. . . . I feel myself to be the greatest ingrate, the vilest rebel in the universe. . . . I must go mad if some changes do not come. How gladly would I redeem the past."

Then he made an appeal for providential direction through the prophetic channel: "O Sister White, will you not for the dear Lord's sake plead with Him for a message for me? Do write to me even if it be only to condemn. Certainty of condemnation would be better than the darkness of uncertainty." [13]

The First Interview

After another eight months of apparent silence, Davis tracked down Ellen White in Sydney, on Thursday, August 5, at the Summer Hill Health Home, where she was staying. In her diary entry for that day there may be an inkling as to one reason (apart from no message from the Lord) she had not written the man earlier:

"I am not able to write. My head will not work. I am compelled to let it rest. Devoted some time to visiting Sister Semmens and Brethren Davis and Semmens." [14]

In a letter to her son, W. C. White, later that day, Ellen referred to this visit with Davis, mentioning that "he has worked very interestedly to get the petitions before the [local municipal] council"—though the council subsequently rejected them. [15] But there was not a hint as to any other matters discussed between them.

Three days later, on Sunday, August 8, Ellen visited again with Davis before returning by train to Cooranbong, three hours distant. For the first time we begin to understand from her pen something of the deeper nature of Davis' problems. For she confided to her diary:

"I had a long conversation with Brother Davis this morning. Poor man, he is in trouble. He once dabbled with spiritualism and theosophy, and its dark influence has shrouded him ever since. Although he sees the truth and believes the truth, yet there seems to be a bondage to this power that is hard for him to break. I could only bid him 'Look and live.' An uplifted Saviour will heal the serpent's bite, and although its poison has been diffused through his entire being, I could say to him, 'Look and live.' Satan has indeed tempted him and desired to sift him as wheat [Luke 22:31, 32], but Christ is a living Saviour and Advocate in the courts of heaven in his behalf. May the Lord deliver him from the cruel power of Satan is my prayer." [16]

Nothing if not persistent, Davis wrote Mrs. White a few days later to tell her that he had been able to reenter the colporteur work, but that he still owed the astronomical (for that day) sum of £250. The publishing house was giving him only 10 percent of his normal commission, applying the remainder to the debt on his outstanding account. Thus, "the yoke of debt that remains on us seems to be simply intolerable."

"When I reentered the canvassing work I feared the result. I told them plainly at the office that I had no confidence in myself; fear and pride prevented me from stating why, and the end is just such as the whole was and has ever been. . . .

"We cannot go on as we are at present. . . . The difficulty now is that I am perfectly nonplussed. I want to do right and to honorably discharge all my liabilities. . . . I want to overcome my vile traits of character and honor my Saviour by my life. But how I am to do it, what course I ought to pursue and what step I ought to take now, I cannot see. . . .

"I am a failure and I fear lest that fact will lead me to utter ruin." [17]

The Second Interview

On Sunday evening, August 15, Davis met again with the prophetess at her home at Cooranbong. After she retired that night Davis's case was opened more fully to her, and at 3:00 a.m. she started a long letter to him that was not completed until several days later.

Three main problems were raised in this letter:

1. *Demon Possession:* Before they parted Sunday evening, Mrs.

White prayed that Davis "might be delivered from the power of satanic agencies that were determined to hold control over you until they should bring you down to their own lowest depths. I advised you to open everything to Elder [A. G.] Daniells and our leading brethren, and solicit their prayers in your behalf, that Satan might be rebuked.

"You answered me that you had not been troubled with the temptations you had when canvassing, that since you had been circulating the petitions you had been free from these horrible temptations. But when we were bowed before God I could see you surrounded with demons, all ready to take you under their control and lead you wherever they chose. . . .

"You cannot break this spell. You have not yet broken it." [18]

The next night she had another dream, and added to her letter: "You are not free from Satan's power to do even the things you purpose to do." [19]

Finally she concluded the letter by stating, "You are under the control of an unclean spirit." "There is only one hope for you. . . . If you determine to break the power of satanic agencies that is upon you, present your case before the servants of God, humble your heart before God, and ask them to pray for you that God will have mercy upon you." [20]

2. *Debts:* Generous soul that she was, Mrs. White stated in her letter that she was about to enclose some money to help Davis ease his debt situation, whereupon the Holy Spirit immediately and emphatically rejected this large-hearted response:

"The Spirit of the Lord teaches me that as you now are, this would be using the Lord's money to hurt yourself and other souls. . . . To trust you with money [at this time] would be to put it into a bag with holes [Haggai 1:6], and you would be no more relieved than before you received it." [21]

She concluded this section with practical advice on how he might extricate himself from this large burden of debt.

3. *Immorality:* There is just the hint of reference to marital infidelity on Davis' part in this interesting letter. She wrote, somewhat obliquely: "You have vile thoughts, and have corrupted your ways before God. . . . Your course is immoral. You are bringing disgrace upon the cause of truth. Whatever may have been your past course of action, you have not been converted to the mind and

character of purity and cleanness and truthfulness before God. . . .
You have brought moral corruption upon souls. You are a dangerous
man to be left to yourself anywhere." [22]

An Amazing Experience

Davis, understandably, was apparently extremely reluctant to
appeal to the leaders of the church to pray for his deliverance, lest he
be obliged to reveal these secret sins.

About this time an amazing experience unfolded one Sabbath
afternoon at a small red brick chapel in North Fitzroy, a suburb of
greater Melbourne. The story was related to me in 1970 by an
eyewitness, Herold M. Blunden, who at that time was but a lad of 12. [23]

Blunden lived in North Fitzroy and was a member of the little
congregation that worshiped in this chapel. [24] He was genuinely
troubled by the presence in their midst of the "American lady
prophet." As he later remembered:

"My pastor believed in her, my Sabbath school class teacher
believed in her, and my parents believed in her. But I couldn't
believe in her just because they did." [25]

Young Herold was particularly bothered by the facts of Mrs.
White's nationality and gender. "Surely," he later recalled in our
interview, "there were enough *Australians* around, that God need
not pick an *American!* And surely there were enough *men* available,
that God need not choose a *woman!*"

But being a somewhat open-minded youth, he decided he would
put her to the test—though, at the moment, he hadn't the slightest
idea of how he would test her! An unexpected opportunity, however,
soon presented itself.

Mrs. White was scheduled to speak one Sabbath afternoon in the
little chapel in North Fitzroy. Herold decided to go early and secure
a seat right down in front, on the aisle of the second row of pews,
from which vantage point he would be able to see and hear
everything. It was in the remarkable providence of God that he did
so.

Coming from Sydney by train, Mrs. White was delayed nearly two
hours. The chapel was "standing room only," and the members
occupied themselves with singing, praying, the giving of personal
testimonies, etc., until she arrived.

Finally she appeared, walking into the chapel on the arm of the young American missionary, Arthur Grosvenor Daniells, president of the Australasian Union Conference (organized just four years earlier). He escorted her to the platform, introduced her, and then retired to one of the two empty seats among the ministers in the center of the rostrum.

Mrs. White carried a sheaf of manuscript in her hand, which she laid upon the pulpit. She adjusted it, adjusted her shawl, looked up at the audience, smiled, and opened her mouth to speak—but nothing came out. She seemed mildly surprised, and scanned her audience from left to right, as if looking for someone in particular.

Then she looked down again, readjusted her manuscript and shawl, looked up, smiled, and opened her mouth to speak—and again no words came forth. This time she began to register concern as well as surprise. She again surveyed her audience, more slowly than at first, looking from one side to the other. But this time she continued to turn her body, the better to view the faces of those seated behind her on the rostrum.

With her back thus to the audience, what she said next could not be heard by worshipers sitting farther back than the first two rows of pews (there being no public address system in those days).

Noticing Nathaniel Davis sitting next to Elder Daniells, she immediately questioned Daniells why Davis was on the same platform with her.

Davis, at six feet five inches, was taller seated than the five-foot-two-inch prophet standing. He rose slowly to his full height, towering above the diminutive prophet. He gave her a most hateful look, turned abruptly upon his heel, and stalked off the platform, down the center aisle, and out of the chapel.

Unperturbed, Mrs. White returned to the pulpit, adjusted her manuscript, adjusted her shawl, looked up at the congregation, smiled, opened her mouth—and this time began speaking. She continued for the next 75 minutes or so.

But young Herold Blunden's mind was in a whirl. "What did all this mean?" he asked himself repeatedly. He never heard a word of the message that day by the "American lady prophet."

When the service was concluded, all in the congregation moved to the door to greet their visiting speaker—all except Herold Blunden. He went, instead, to the rostrum to inquire from Elder Daniells as to what this all might mean. This is what he discovered:

Nathaniel Davis had a problem with money, women, and spiritualism. Davis had been told to ask his fellow clergy to pray for his deliverance from demonic possession, but apparently thus far he had declined. Therefore, sitting on the rostrum that Sabbath afternoon, he was a living, visible representative of the kingdom of darkness. And, as Ellen White would often affirm, "this work is of God, or it is not. God does nothing in partnership with Satan. . . . The testimonies are of the Spirit of God, or of the devil." [26]

God would not loosen His prophet's tongue to speak until this representative of the kingdom of darkness had departed!

Young Blunden, intending somehow to test the prophet, had never bargained for *this* kind of test!

Ellen White Appeals for Help

Since Davis would not initiate contact with church leaders for assistance, Mrs. White next urged Daniells to approach the errant church worker to explore measures for his deliverance from satanic bondage. On August 31, 1897, she wrote the president:

"Evil angels are all about him, and at times have control of him in a strange, revolting way. . . . I have the word from the Lord that he is possessed of an evil spirit, and 'has no power from the snare to go.' His case is like the cases of ancient times. At times, he thinks, speaks, and acts under the influence of satanic agencies, and does revolting things. This casts him into despair. His only hope is to present his case before his brethren who have a living connection with God. The spell will be broken only by the most earnest wrestling with God, and this I present to you. . . . As soon as possible, this demon tempter's power must be broken. . . . Satan must be rebuked as in olden time, in the name of Jesus Christ of Nazareth. This in faith we must ask the Lord to do, and He will fulfill His word. The Lord will hear prayer. . . . Labor we must to have the man dispossessed." [27]

The next day Ellen wrote a letter jointly to Elder Daniells and four other church leaders, reflecting her continuing concern that "people will be tested and proved, as in the case of Brother Davis and in the case of Sister Miller. God's servants need constantly to lay hold of souls ready to perish with one hand, while with the hand of faith they lay hold of the throne of God. Souls possessed of evil spirits will present themselves before us. We must cultivate the spirit of earnest prayer mingled with genuine faith to save them from ruin; and all the relief gained will confirm our faith." [28]

Mrs. White followed up that letter with a letter of counsel to Davis on September 2, but sent it to Daniells, [29] asking the latter to read the epistle to Davis at the earliest possible moment.

Daniells' Visit With Davis

Sensing that time was of the essence, Daniells traveled to Ballarat immediately, on the return swing from a trip to Adelaide, intending to devote his weekend there to efforts in counseling Davis.

A meeting was arranged at Davis's home on Friday evening following a service at the local church. Davis's wife was present. As Daniells later recalled, before an audience of Australian church leaders in New South Wales:

"When I began reading it to him, he became very much excited. After a little, I heard some sort of disturbance, and looking up, saw him with an open knife in his raised hand. I asked, 'What is the matter?' He grated his teeth and glared at me like a madman.

"His wife and I appealed to him to put the knife down, but he was menacing us so wildly that I did not dare to go on reading. I did not know whether he would thrust it into me or his wife or himself. I said, 'Let us kneel down and pray to God. There is a God in Israel who can help us, and we must have His help.'

"We knelt down, and I may tell you that I was never in a more perplexing place. I knew that demons were in the room and I knew that we must have the power of that same Christ who subdued demons and cast out devils while among men.

"The first thing I said was 'O Lord, we come to Thee in the all-prevailing name of Jesus.' At the mention of the name Jesus, that man hurled his knife across the room with terrible violence. At the mention of the all-powerful name of Jesus he broke into sobs and the violence disappeared. After his wife and I had prayed, he prayed most earnestly to God to deliver him from those tormenting devils.

"When we arose I finished reading the message, and then asked him to tell us what he knew about the truthfulness of this message. I had not known anything of this before.

"He said, 'Brother Daniells, every word of it is true. For weeks I have been tormented by these evil spirits. I have been thrown out of my bed, and I have been hammered on the floor by those demons; it has wrecked my nerves, and I was about to give up to them and become their obedient slave again.' " [30]

Writing to Mrs. White a more complete account of what transpired, on September 12, 1897, Daniells said that Davis "described
the spirit that had followed him. . . . It purports to be the spirit of an
Oriental from Tibet. This spirit has appeared to Brother Davis over
and over again. He has a white beard and wears a turban. . . . The last
time this spirit appeared to him . . . Brother Davis had just gone to
bed when it approached him with a terrible countenance. On
reaching the bedside, it laid one hand upon him, and raised the other
hand and swore that he would kill him. Brother Davis cried out in
agony, and it left. He says that the awful visage of that spirit remained
in his mind so that he could hardly sleep that night. It seemed to him
that if it appeared to him again, it would surely end his life." [31]

Daniells also described the experience when he uttered the name
of Jesus in his prayer of deliverance:

"We bowed down, and the moment I mentioned the name of
Christ, the room seemed flooded with the presence of the divine
Being. I do not think I ever experienced anything like it in connection with other persons. I have a few times when alone felt the
wonderful presence of God as I did that night, but I do not remember
ever having done so in company . . . [with any] one else. We all
realized in a moment that Christ was in the room, and that Satan's
power was broken. . . . We could do nothing but praise the Lord. We
did not have to ask Him to rebuke the enemy, for we knew that Jesus
was there, and that Satan had left us. . . . There was no question with
us but what our Saviour was standing in the room." [32]

Daniells then gave his own reaction to all that had transpired:

"I have always shrunk from meeting the devil in that form, and
have dreaded the idea of having to rebuke Satan. But when I saw how
the mention of the name of Christ in living faith broke the power of
the enemy, scattered his darkness, and filled our hearts with light and
joy and peace, I received new impressions in regard to meeting the
power of the enemy." [33]

The president concluded his letter to Mrs. White with this
observation:

"The Lord has shown Himself ready to give the man complete
deliverance. It rests altogether with Brother Davis himself. If he will
believe God and abide in Him, he will be a free man. I shall write to
him at once, urging him to be very careful not to lose the Saviour a

single day. If he does, he will lose the blessing he has received. If you have any further light on his case I shall be very glad to receive it." [34]

On October 10, 1897, Davis wrote to inform Mrs. White of the birth of another child the day previously, to ask for a personal copy of the testimony that Daniells had read to them, and to report: "Now I have a continual experience of the presence and communion of heavenly intelligences stimulating my love for truth and righteousness and cheering me in the blessed hope of present victory and future rapture. Both my wife and I are rejoicing in this liberty." [35]

The Denouement

There is no further record of correspondence between Davis and Mrs. White; but exactly three years later, on August 6, 1900, Davis penned a personal note that seems to indicate his—and God's— triumph over the forces of evil in his life.

As Mrs. White made preparation for permanent return to the United States, a group of her friends and associates procured an attractive autograph album. In it they wrote daily messages for her to peruse on board ship. Each communication was prefaced by a full page devoted to the date of the intended reading, accompanied by an artist's attractive sketch illustrating some facet of shipboard life.

The *Moana* left Sydney harbor on Wednesday, August 29, 1900. [36] Exactly seven days into the voyage, on September 5, Ellen White opened the album for that day's greeting. It had been penned on August 6 and was signed "N. A. Davis." Her heart must have been greatly cheered—and relieved—to read his testimonial:

"It affords me the most sincere pleasure to have the privilege of putting on record my appreciation of Sister E. G. White's work and my gratitude to my heavenly Father for the messages sent through her to His people.

"The faithful witness, thus bourne, revealed to me the means whereby the bondage of Satan was broken when, owing to the influence of spiritualism, I had well nigh become a spiritual wreck.

"I have every reason to be positive in my confidence in Sister E. G. White as a true prophet.

"May the Lord of love and mercy, grace and truth, guide and guard her safely to the end, and lengthen her days so that she may continue to warn, admonish, and strengthen the remnant people of

God." [37]

Conclusion

God—and His prophets—*do* care about individual persons, and have spent a substantial amount of their collective time in responding to their needs over the millennia. The words of King Jehoshaphat, first uttered about 850 B.C., are as true today as then: "Believe in the Lord your God, so shall ye be established; believe his prophets, so shall ye prosper" (2 Chron. 20:20).

Notes and References

[1] COL 187.

[2] DA 479, 480.

[3] SC 100.

[4] CS 136.

[5] *Ibid.,* p. 135; cf. Ev 359; 5T 507; 6T 148, 264, 446; TM 84, 454.

[6] 1T 345, 346.

[7] Herold M. Blunden, "Guidance for Earth's Last Generations," annual Spirit of Prophecy Emphasis Day sermon, Apr. 12, 1958, p. 7.

[8] Letter 36, 1897, pp. 1-3.

[9] Nathaniel Davis to Ellen G. White, Sept. 9, 1896, p. 1.

[10] *Ibid.,* pp. 5, 7.

[11] *Ibid.,* p. 8.

[12] *Ibid.,* pp. 2, 4, 5.

[13] *Ibid.,* Dec. 18, 1896, pp. 1-5.

[14] Ms 175, 1897, p. 4.

[15] Letter 195, 1897, p. 1.

[16] Ms 175, 1897, p. 6.

[17] Nathaniel Davis to Ellen G. White, Aug. 12, 1897, pp. 1, 2.

[18] Letter 36, 1897, p. 1.

[19] *Ibid.,* p. 2.

[20] *Ibid.,* pp. 2-4.

[21] *Ibid.,* p. 2.

[22] *Ibid.,* pp. 2, 3.

[23] Personal interview with Herold M. Blunden, Crystal Springs Manor, Deer Park, California. Unfortunately, the date of this interview was not properly recorded at the time. I have reason to believe it took place in early 1970, four years before his death in 1974 (see obituary, *Review and Herald,* Oct. 24, 1974). Blunden himself recorded some of the incidents related in this interview, though without indicating he himself was an eyewitness, in his sermon cited above.

[24] This structure still stands today, and is regarded as the oldest South Pacific Division Seventh-day Adventist church building still located on its original site. I visited there during a service Sabbath afternoon, October 26, 1985.

[25] Blunden interview.

[26] 4T 230.

[27] Letter 39, Aug. 31, 1897, pp. 6, 7.

[28] Letter 49, 1897, p. 5.

[29] Ms 176, 1897, p. 2.

[30] Ministerial Institute address, June 25, 1928; transcript in *Australasian Record,* Aug. 13, 1928.

[31] A. G. Daniells to Ellen G. White, Sept. 12, 1897, p. 2. Received by Mrs. White three days later (Ms 176, 1897, p. 16). Note: Daniells evidently typed this letter himself, as it is filled with numerous strikeovers and typographical errors. I have here corrected the text, also adding capitalization to references to the Deity, lest the reader become distracted by the clutter that would be caused by reproducing an exact transcript with each typographical error faithfully noted. Incidentally, Daniells, interestingly, does not mention Davis'

knife-throwing incident in this letter, though he does refer to it in his 1928 remarks back in Australia.

[32] *Ibid.,* pp. 1, 2.

[33] *Ibid.,* p. 3.

[34] *Ibid.,* p. 4. Davis also wrote a 10-page letter to Mrs. White relating details of Daniells' interview with him at Ballarat. He incorrectly dates it as August 5; in all probability it should have been dated September 5.

[35] Nathaniel Davis to Ellen White, Oct. 10, 1897, p. 1.

[36] 4Bio 457.

[37] Dated at Geelong (a suburb of Melbourne), Victoria, Australia. The White Estate still has in its possession this interesting artifact.

CHAPTER 9

THE "BALLS OF FIRE" VISIONS
"The Destruction"

July 1, 1904 / August 24, 1906

THEOLOGY has been defined as the study of God, and theologians of analytical bent have systematized this inquiry by dividing it into component subspecializations, much as a housewife might cut a pie into a number of wedge-shaped slices before serving.

For example, Christology deals with the doctrine of God in Christ. Pneumatology is concerned with the doctrine of the Holy Spirit. Soteriology focuses upon the doctrine of salvation. Eschatology examines the doctrine of "last things," and so on.

Seventh-day Adventists, from earliest times, have had a compelling, even a consuming, interest in eschatology. Indeed, their corporate name draws attention to two of their chief ("pillar") doctrines — the seventh-day Sabbath and the second coming of the Lord of the Sabbath.

When John the Baptist (and subsequently, Jesus Himself) proclaimed that "the kingdom of heaven is at hand" (Matt. 3:2; 4:17; 10:7), reference was primarily being made to what theologians have called "the Kingdom of grace," instituted at the Fall of man in Eden and confirmed or established at Calvary. [1]

"The kingdom of glory," on the other hand, will be ushered in at the second coming of Jesus. At that time "the kingdoms of this world are become the kingdoms of our Lord, and of his Christ; and he shall reign for ever and ever" (Rev. 11:15). "When the Son of man shall come in his glory, and all the holy angels with him, then shall he sit upon the throne of his glory: and before him shall be gathered all nations" (Matt. 25:31, 32).

The second coming of Christ, but dimly foreseen in the Old Testament, is a preeminent doctrine of the New. It is a subject of promise and prophecy. Just before His crucifixion, upon the night of betrayal, Jesus promised His disciples that He would "go and prepare a place for you"; and then later "I will come again, and receive you unto myself; that where I am, there ye may be also" (John 14:3).

The "gospel of the kingdom" must first be "preached in all the world for a witness unto all nations; and then shall the end come" (Matt. 24:14).

Some 60 years after Christ ascended to heaven, He returned briefly to share a "revelation" of Himself and of the future with His beloved friend, John Zebedee. The disciple-become-prophet had been banished by Emperor Domitian to the Isle of Patmos for preaching the gospel.

Three times in the final chapter of the last book of the Bible, Jesus promised to return: "Behold, I come quickly." "Behold, I come quickly." "Surely, I come quickly" (Rev. 22:7, 12, 20). Whereupon John offered the closing prayer of the New Testament, "Even so, come, Lord Jesus" (Rev. 22:20).

The Second Coming was a favorite theme of New Testament writers. Paul declared "the glorious appearing of the great God and our Saviour Jesus Christ" to be "that blessed hope" (Titus 2:13). And five times in three of his epistles he spoke longingly, lovingly of "that day" (1 Thess. 5:4; 2 Thess. 2:3; 2 Tim. 1:12; 1:18; 4:8).

Jesus Himself informed us that there would be a painfully acute trauma connected with the scenes of earth's history immediately prior to His return. There would be, He declared solemnly, "great tribulation, such as was not since the beginning of the world to this time, no, nor ever shall be" (Matt. 24:21). There would also be a concomitant "distress of nations" and "men's hearts failing them for fear, and for looking after those things which are coming on the earth" (Luke 21:25, 26).

The apostle Peter declared that this "day of the Lord" would be accompanied by the "heavens" passing away "with a great noise, and the elements shall melt with fervent heat, the earth also and the works that are therein shall be burned up." Indeed, the heavens "being on fire shall be dissolved, and the elements shall melt with fervent heat" (2 Peter 3:10, 12).

John adds, ominously, in the Revelation that one of the primary purposes of the second coming of Jesus will be to "destroy them which destroy the earth" (Rev. 11:18).

Truly "that day" will be preceded by "a time of trouble, such as never was since there was a nation even to that same time" (Dan. 12:1).

Two Amazing Visions

In our own time Ellen White was given a view of final, end-time events. Her most complete scenario is to be found in her book *The Great Controversy,* as we have noted in chapter 5.

But not all the important events are therein described. Two of her most interesting and significant visions (in view of our present-day knowledge of nuclear physics) are to be found in other works.

1. On Friday night, July 1, 1904, at Nashville, Tennessee, Ellen White was given a view of apocalyptic doom. The next morning, toward the close of a sermon in the chapel of the Southern Publishing Association, she made a brief, if oblique, reference to it: "Last night a scene was presented before me. I may never feel free to reveal all of it, but I will reveal a little." [2]

Four months later, writing in the *Review and Herald,* she elaborated upon this "very impressive scene":

"I saw an immense ball of fire falling among some beautiful mansions, causing their instant destruction. I heard someone say, 'We knew that the judgments of God were coming upon the earth, but we did not know that they would come so soon.' Others said, 'You knew? Why then did you not tell us? We did not know.' On every side I heard such words spoken." [3]

2. Two years later, at Sanitarium [St. Helena], California, in the early-morning hours of Friday, August 24, 1906, she had a similar dream. Again she characterized it as "a very impressive scene" of "a terrible conflagration." [4] In her diary that morning she wrote:

"In the night I was, I thought, in a room not in my own house. I was in a city, where I knew not, and I heard expression after expression. I rose up quickly in bed, and saw from my window large balls of fire. Jetting out were sparks, in the form of arrows, and buildings were being consumed, and in a very few minutes the entire block of buildings was falling and the screeching and mournful groans came distinctly to my ears. I cried out, in my raised position, to learn what was happening. . . . Then I awoke. But I could not tell where I was, for I was in another place than home. I said, O Lord, where am I and what shall I do? It was as a voice that spoke, 'Be not afraid. Nothing shall harm you.'

"I was instructed that destruction had gone forth upon cities. The word of the Lord will be fulfilled. Isaiah 29:19-24 was repeated. I dared not move, not knowing where I was. I cried unto the Lord, What does it mean? These representations of destruction were repeated. Where am I? [Said the Lord,] 'In scenes I have represented that which will be; but warn My people to cease from putting their trust in men who are not obedient to My warnings and who despise My reproof, for the day of the Lord is right upon the world when evidence shall be made sure. Those who have followed the voices that would turn things upside down will themselves be turned where they cannot see, but will be as blind men.'

"These words were given me from Isaiah 30: [verses 8-15 quoted]." [5]

Three days later, in making reference to these words, she added: "I was instructed that light had been given me and that I had written under special light the Lord had imparted." [6]

Writing to her son, W. C. White, on August 27, Mrs. White added, concerning these "fiery arrows" that "were flying in every direction" from these multiple "balls of fire": "It was impossible to check the fires that were kindled, and many places were being destroyed. The terror of the people was indescribable. After a time I awoke and found myself at home."

She concluded the letter with this cryptic remark: "I have had many things opened to me, but it is not my duty to reveal all that will surely come to those who manifest a spirit to walk contrary to the way God has marked out for them. Everyone will be rewarded as his work shall be." [7]

Were these "balls of fire," which Ellen White witnessed twice in the space of two years, thermonuclear explosions? It is impossible today to give a dogmatic answer. But a "ball of fire" is one of the most obvious identifying characteristics of atomic explosions—of which the first man-made one was yet some 40 years in the future!

On July 16, 1945, elements literally did "melt with fervent heat" in a spectacular predawn explosion when the first atomic bomb was experimentally detonated on the white sands of the desert near Alamogordo, New Mexico. The highly secret "Manhattan Project" was a success. And though that first A-bomb was crude by standards of measurement a half century later, it nevertheless exploded with a force of 20,000 tons of TNT! [8]

Less than one month afterward, on August 6, 1945, a B-29 bomber, the *Enola Gay,* dropped a similar device over Hiroshima, Japan. Exploding over the city at a height of 600 meters, this bomb killed 70,000 people, injured almost as many more, and flattened nearly five square miles of the city.

Three days later, on August 9, a much more advanced A-bomb was dropped on Nagasaki, killing 40,000, injuring another 40,000, and destroying one and one-half square miles. The result was that World War II came to a precipitous halt. [9]

Hiroshima in 1985

Four decades later, on March 31, 1985, I visited Hiroshima to conduct meetings for ministers and members in the local Seventh-day Adventist church. During a break, I was escorted downtown to an exceptionally large grassy park, "Ground Zero." All that stood there were the ruins of one building (the "atomic dome"), in a fenced enclosure over on one edge of the park. Its grotesquely twisted steel girders angrily stabbed the sky; in the center of the park was a large rectangular Peace Memorial Museum, raised up perhaps 30 feet above the pavement on concrete "stilts."

Inside I learned that the first A-bomb killed and destroyed in three ways: (1) the heat from the fireball literally vaporized steel and concrete within a radius of several miles (the apostle Peter spoke of last-day elements melting from "fervent heat"); (2) the concussion from the detonation flattened thousands of reinforced steel structures (again, Peter said the heavens would pass away "with a great noise"); and (3) deadly radiation burned and contaminated everything for miles around.

I felt as if I were standing where the end of the world began!

Hiroshima and Nagasaki were not, however, the first cities in history to be destroyed by "balls of fire."

Writing from Europe in the *Review and Herald* in 1886, Mrs. White described the destruction of Sodom and the cities of the plain (see Gen. 19:29), about 1900 B.C., in this graphic depiction:

"As the sun arose for the last time upon the cities of the plain, the people thought to commence another day of godless riot. All were eagerly planning their business or their pleasure, and the messenger of God was derided for his fears and his warnings. Suddenly as the thunder peal from an unclouded sky fell balls of fire on the doomed capital."

Then immediately Ellen White made this stunning application to the end of the world: " 'So shall also the coming of the Son of man be.' The people will be eating and drinking, planting and building, marrying and giving in marriage, until the wrath of God shall be poured out without mixture of mercy. The world will be rocked to sleep in the cradle of carnal security." [10]

If, indeed, I had stood where "the end of the world began," and if nuclear destruction is to be a part and parcel of the climax of events just preceding the Second Coming, then Mrs. White's assurances for Christians, in this context, must be especially appreciated and encouraging.

For, she declares, while the ninety-first psalm ("a thousand shall fall at thy side, and ten thousand at thy right hand; but it shall not come nigh thee") has been the refuge of God's people in every age during the 3,000 years since David first reduced it to writing, yet it has a special application to those who live just before the close of probation: [11]

"In the ninety-first psalm is a most wonderful description of *the coming of the Lord* to bring the wickedness of the wicked to an end, and to give to those who have chosen Him as their Redeemer the assurance of His love and protecting care." [12]

How interested and excited I was, then, while eating my last meal in Hiroshima at our church (built after the atomic devastation of August 6, 1945), when the local church elder responded to our question "How many Seventh-day Adventists died in that first atomic blast in 1945?" As this Japanese Christian leader looked at us, his eyes began to brim with tears and he answered softly through an interpreter, "Not one!"

Yes, some experienced radiation burns; most lost their houses and all earthly possessions. But *not one Seventh-day Adventist* lost his or her life! The promise was sure: "It shall not come nigh thee. Only with thine eyes shalt thou behold and see. . . . There shall no evil befall thee, neither shall any plague come nigh thy dwelling. For he shall give his angels charge over thee, to keep thee in all thy ways.

They shall bear thee up in their hands, lest thou dash thy foot against a stone" (Ps. 91:7-12).

Appeal to Get Ready

Particularly during the final two decades of her 87-year life, Ellen White continued to express concern for the inhabitants of wicked cities, who needed to be warned from the wrath to come; and for God's people, who needed to complete successfully the work of personal preparation for the great day of the Lord.

As early as 1888, she hinted at what was yet to come: "The Saviour's prophecy concerning the visitation of judgments upon Jerusalem is to have another fulfillment, of which that terrible desolation was but a faint shadow. In the fate of the chosen city we may behold the doom of a world that has rejected God's mercy and trampled upon His law." [13]

Just after the turn of the century, in 1903, she enlarged more fully upon this situation with these words: "The present is a time of overwhelming interest to all living. Rulers and statesmen, men who occupy positions of trust and authority, thinking men and women of all classes, have their attention fixed upon the events taking place about us. They are watching the strained, restless relations that exist among the nations. They observe the intensity that is taking possession of every earthly element, and they recognize that something great and decisive is about to take place—that the world is on the verge of a stupendous crisis.

"Angels are now restraining the winds of strife, that they may not blow until the world shall be warned of its coming doom; but a storm is gathering, ready to burst upon the earth; and when God shall bid His angels loose the winds, there will be such a scene of strife as no pen can picture." [14]

And, again, later that same year: "O that God's people had a sense of the impending destruction of thousands of cities, now almost given to idolatry!" [15]

Six years later, in 1909, she described a vision she had received at Loma Linda, California, on April 16 of that year: "During a vision of the night, I stood on an eminence, from which I could see houses shaken like a reed in the wind. Buildings, great and small, were falling to the ground. Pleasure resorts, theaters, hotels, and the homes of the wealthy were shaken and shattered. Many lives were blotted out of existence, and the air was filled with the shrieks of the injured and the terrified.

"The destroying angels . . . were at work. One touch, and buildings, so thoroughly constructed that men regarded them as secure against every danger, quickly became heaps of rubbish. There was no assurance of safety in any place. I did not feel in any special peril, but the awfulness of the scenes that passed before me I cannot find words to describe. It seemed that the forbearance of God was exhausted and that the judgment day had come.

"The angel that stood by my side then instructed me that but few have any conception of the wickedness existing in our world today, especially the wickedness in the large cities. He declared that the Lord has appointed a time when He will visit transgressors in wrath for persistent disregard of His law." [16]

The next year she wrote: "The time is near when large cities will be swept away, and all should be warned of these coming judgments." [17]

She voiced an appeal to Christians within her own church not only to warn the wicked, but also to prepare their own lives, that they might meet the appearance of Jesus with peace in their hearts and a smile upon their faces:

"Soon grievous troubles will arise among the nations—trouble that will not cease until Jesus comes. As never before we need to press together, serving Him who has prepared His throne in the heavens and whose kingdom ruleth over all. God has not forsaken His people, and our strength lies in not forsaking Him.

"The judgments of God are in the land. The wars and rumors of wars, the destruction by fire and flood, say clearly that the time of trouble, which is to increase until the end, is very near at hand. We have no time to lose." [18]

God's Final Work

Finally, employing an interesting metephor, she spoke of the special work of the heavenly angels during the "sealing time," concerning which most Christians were unaware: "Satan is now using every device in this sealing time to keep the minds of God's people from the present truth and to cause them to waver. I saw a covering that God was drawing over His people to protect them in the time of trouble; and every soul that was decided on the truth and was pure in heart was to be covered with the covering of the Almighty.

"Satan knew this, and he was at work in mighty power to keep the minds of as many people as he possibly could wavering and unsettled on the truth. . . . I saw that Satan was at work in these ways to distract, deceive, and draw away God's people, just now in this sealing time.

"I saw some who were not standing stiffly for present truth. Their knees were trembling, and their feet sliding, because they were not firmly planted on the truth, and the covering of Almighty God could not be drawn over them while they were thus trembling.

"Satan was trying his every art to hold them where they were, until the sealing was past, until the covering was drawn over God's people, and they were left without a shelter from the burning wrath of God, in the seven last plagues.

"God has begun to draw this covering over His people, and it will soon be drawn over all who are to have a shelter in the day of slaughter. God will work in power for His people; and Satan will be permitted to work also." [19]

Conclusion

To us today comes an ancient appeal, but in a most contemporary setting. The apostle Peter implores those living in that end-time day, when elements "melt with fervent heat": "Since, then, all these things are to be melted away, what kind of persons ought you to be in holy behavior and godliness?" (see 2 Peter 3:11).

"For this reason, loved ones, since you are looking for these things, be careful to be found by Him in peace, without spot and without blame" (see verse 14).

Things will be so bad in the final days before Jesus returns that the primary question of even the wicked will be: "The great day of his wrath is come; *and who shall be able to stand?*" (Rev. 6:17).

Ironically, their question is but the echo of an ancient psalm, sung antiphonally by the Israelites as they journeyed three times each year to the annual national feasts. As they climbed the steep ascent from the Jericho plain (800 feet below sea level) to Jerusalem, on Mount Zion (2,500 feet above sea level), one group would sing to the other:

"Who shall ascend into the hill of the Lord? Or who shall stand in His holy place?"

And the answer would come from the other group:

"He that hath clean hands, and a pure heart; who hath not lifted up his soul unto vanity, nor sworn deceitfully. He shall receive the blessing from the Lord, and righteousness from the God of his salvation" (Ps. 24:3-5).

"Then said Jesus . . . Go and do thou likewise" (Luke 10:37). "What I say unto you I say unto all; Watch" (Mark 13:37). "He that hath an ear, let him hear what the Spirit saith unto the churches" (Rev. 2:7, 11, 17, 29; 3:6, 13, 22; 13:9).

Notes and References

[1] GC 347, 348.
[2] Ms 102, 1904, p. 9.
[3] RH, Nov. 24, 1904; cf. 9T 28, 29.
[4] Letter 278, 1906, p. 1; cited in Ev 29.
[5] Ms 126, 1908, p. 2.
[6] *Ibid.*, p. 5.
[7] Letter 278, 1906, p. 2; cited in Ev 29.
[8] *World Book Encyclopedia* (1960), vol. 1, p. 710.
[9] *Ibid.*, p. 713.
[10] RH, Oct. 26, 1886; cited in 5BC 1122.
[11] 3BC 843.
[12] Ms 151 1901, p. 3; cited in 3BC 1150. (Italics supplied.)
[13] GC 36.
[14] Ed 179, 180.
[15] RH, Sept. 10, 1903.
[16] 9T 92.
[17] Ms 53, 1910, p. 2; cited in WM 135 and Ev 29.
[18] RH, Nov. 24, 1904; cited in WM 136.
[19] EW 43, 44.

CHAPTER 10

THE "MOVING INTO LINE" VISION
"THE UNITY"

1913

THE thirty-eighth session of the General Conference was scheduled to convene in Takoma Park, Maryland, a growing suburb of Washington, D.C., from May 15 to June 8, 1913. The Seventh-day Adventist Church world headquarters had been relocated here from Battle Creek, Michigan, in 1903, as had the Review and Herald publishing enterprise, both at the instance of Ellen White. [1]

The following year, 1904, the Adventist presence in Takoma Park had been augmented by the establishment of Washington Training College, known today as Columbia Union College. [2] It was on the 20-acre campus of the college that a large tent was pitched in 1913, to accommodate the 372 delegates expected to attend the session. [3]

Sessions were now held every four years. From the founding of the General Conference in 1863 until 1889, sessions had been held annually, then biennially until 1905. [4]

After her return from Australia, Ellen White had attended and addressed the sessions of 1901, 1903, 1905, and 1909. [5] The latter session was the last at which she personally appeared. Her parting words to the delegates upon this occasion—actually a postscript to her sermon—were spoken as she held aloft her Bible: "Brethren and sisters, I commend unto you this Book." [6]

Now, in 1913, too feeble to make the arduous journey from her Elmshaven home in northern California, she had to settle for sending a written message of greeting and counsel by the hand of her son, W. C. White. [7] This was the last General Conference session she addressed; she died on July 16, 1915.

The brief eight-paragraph letter was addressed to "My dear Brethren." She began, typically, by encouraging the delegates to "cherish a spirit of hopefulness and courage." Always positive in word and tone, she urged her brethren to focus their attention upon Christ, to daily "be endowed . . . with a rich measure of His Holy Spirit," to seek deeper consecration, and to consider carefully and seriously "the times in which we are living," in the context of the soon return of Jesus.

The exhortation concluded with these stirring words: "I have been deeply impressed by scenes that have recently passed before me in the night season. There seemed to be a great movement—a work of revival—going forward in many places. *Our people were moving into line,* responding to God's call. My brethren, the Lord is speaking to us. Shall we not heed His voice? Shall we not trim our lamps, and act like men who look for their Lord to come? The time is one that calls for light bearing, for action." [8]

"Our people were moving into line."

What did she mean by this interesting metaphor? Was she referring to what the British call a "queue"—a line of people waiting to board a bus, or to be served in a bank or post office? Hardly.

Several paragraphs earlier she had spoken of the importance of church workers being "on the Lord's side"—an obvious reference to the great controversy between Christ and Satan. In this military motif she added, "I see a crisis before us, and the Lord calls for His laborers to come into line." [9] Into a military-like line of march, a line of battle. God's people were called to present a united front against the enemy.

This expression must be seen in the context of the great "sifting" or "shaking" [10] that would decimate the church just before the close of probation, with a "great proportion" [11] of its members (as then constituted) abandoning the remnant church. But while many would leave, others—under the influence of the "latter rain" of the Holy Spirit—would come in to take their places. There would be no diminution of numbers, and the church would then prepare for its final conflict with Satan and evil. [12]

It is this *purified, unified* church that she now beheld "coming into line."

A Compelling Preoccupation

A survey of the published writings of Ellen White reveals that she used the word "unity" 1,666 times and the word "union" 2,269 times. The subject of Christian unity was, for her, a compelling preoccupation and a continuing concern throughout her entire ministry. [13]

She dwelt frequently upon the unity between the Father and the Son of God in heaven, [14] repeatedly holding it up as an ideal for Christians to follow upon the earth. [15] She spoke often of the need for unity between Christ and His followers, [16] and referred to Christ's prayer for unity in the church in the seventeenth chapter of John's Gospel at least 50 times. [17] She stated that that prayer (the longest recorded of Christ in Scripture) should be the creed of the Seventh-day Adventist Church. [18]

Specifically, Mrs. White saw the need of Christian unity:

● Among Seventh-day Adventist church members [19] of varied dispositions [20] and different nationalities. [21]

● Between various Seventh-day Adventist church congregations. [22]

● Among ministers and various gospel workers. [23]

● Among physicians, [24] and between physicians and ministers. [25]

● Between medical missionaries and gospel ministers, [26] and other Seventh-day Adventist church workers. [27]

● Among denominational institutional workers generally, [28] and especially between sanitarium workers and school workers. [29]

● Between the church's several publishing houses, [30] and among the writers for Seventh-day Adventist publications. [31]

● Indeed, between all departments in God's cause. [32]

● Last but certainly not least, in the Seventh-day Adventist home circle. [33]

That Mrs. White should dwell so largely upon this subject is not surprising, given the substantial emphasis in Scripture itself.

In Psalm 133, for example, David extols unity with a metaphor that probably falls strangely upon the modern ear: "Behold, how good and how pleasant it is for brethren to dwell together in unity! It is like the precious ointment upon the head, that ran down upon the beard, even Aaron's beard: that went down to the skirts of his garments; as the dew of Hermon, and as the dew that descended upon the mountains of Zion: for there the Lord commanded the blessing, even life for evermore."

Early in the New Testament, in the fourth chapter of Paul's Epistle to the Christians at Ephesus, the apostle urged them to endeavor "to keep the unity of the Spirit in the bond of peace" (verse 3): "Till we all come in the unity of the faith, and of the knowledge of the Son of God, unto a perfect [literally, "full-grown"] man, unto the measure of the stature of the fulness of Christ: that we henceforth be no more children, tossed to and fro, and carried about with every wind of doctrine, by the sleight of men, and cunning craftiness, whereby they lie in wait to deceive; but speaking the truth in love, may grow up into him in all things, which is the head, even Christ" (verses 13-15).

Satan's Ultimate Snare

In 1884 Mrs. White wrote of something she could only have witnessed in vision, for she places in direct quotation marks nine paragraphs of Satan's "earnest" counsels to his evil angels regarding "snares" that they were to lay in the path of God's people as they approach "the perils of the last days."

As the chief architect of all evil saw it, "the most successful plan of overthrowing their faith" involved, first of all, an attack on the seventh-day Sabbath; for Satan himself clearly saw it as "the great question which is to decide the destiny of souls." [34]

Satan elaborated upon his strategy of exalting a substitute, counterfeit Sabbath (Sunday), and his plan to use "popular ministers" to proclaim it. "But," he went on, "our principal concern is to silence this sect of Sabbathkeepers"—Seventh-day Adventists! [35]

This would be done, variously, by exciting "popular indignation" against them, enforcing laws ("most severe and exacting") against Sabbathkeeping, and ultimately enacting "a law to exterminate all who will not submit to our authority."

"But before proceeding to these extreme measures," Satan went on, "we must exert all our wisdom and subtlety to deceive and ensnare those who honor the true Sabbath. We can separate many from Christ by worldliness, lust, and pride. They may think themselves safe because they believe the truth, but indulgence of appetite or the lower passions, which will confuse judgment and destroy discrimination, will cause their fall.

"Go, make the possessors of lands and money drunk with the cares of this life. Present the world before them in its most attractive light, that they may lay up their treasure here and fix their affections upon earthly things. We must do our utmost to prevent those who labor in God's cause from obtaining means to use against us. Keep the money in our own ranks. . . . Make them care more for money than for the upbuilding of Christ's kingdom and the spread of the truths we hate, and we need not fear their influence; for we know that every selfish, covetous person will fall under our power, and will finally be separated from God's people." [36]

Then Satan addressed his evil angels on how to recruit helpers from those within the church:

"Through those that have a form of godliness but know not the power, we can gain many who would otherwise do us harm. Lovers of pleasure more than lovers of God will be our most effective helpers. Those of this class who are apt and intelligent will serve as decoys to draw others into our snares. Many will not fear their influence, because they profess the same faith. We will thus lead them to conclude that the requirements of Christ are less strict than they once believed, and that by conformity to the world they would exert a greater influence with worldlings. Thus they will separate from Christ; then they will have no strength to resist our power, and erelong they will be ready to ridicule their former zeal and devotion." [37]

Satan next turned his attention to the proclamation of God's Word in services of corporate worship:

"Until the great decisive blow shall be struck, our efforts against commandment keepers must be untiring. We must be present at all their gatherings. In their large meetings especially our cause will suffer much, and we must exercise great vigilance, and employ all our seductive arts to prevent souls from hearing the truth and becoming impressed by it." [38]

Then Satan developed a two-pronged attack upon truth. First, efforts would be made to subvert truth by false prophets and false teachers: "I will have upon the ground, as my agents, men holding false doctrines mingled with just enough truth to deceive souls." Second, there would be a decided attack against the writings of God's special messenger to the remnant church in the last days—Ellen G. White herself! Continuing the quotation:

"I will also have unbelieving ones present who will express doubts in regard to the Lord's messages of warning to His church. Should the people read and believe these admonitions, we could have little hope of overcoming them. But if we can divert their attention from these warnings, they will remain ignorant of our power and cunning, and we shall secure them in our ranks at last. God will not permit His words to be slighted with impunity. If we can keep souls deceived for a time, God's mercy will be withdrawn, and He will give them up to our full control." [39]

Six years later, in 1890, Ellen White revealed another facet of Satan's strategy to destroy the impact of her inspired writings: the devil would (1) seek to destroy the credibility of the prophet herself within the church, and (2) seek to kindle a hatred against her writings that she characterized as "satanic"—satanic in its origin and satanic in its intensity. [40]

Finally, as the *ultimate* weapon, Satan concluded his strategy session with his fallen angels with these cogent, trenchant words:

"We must cause distraction and division. We must destroy their anxiety for their own souls, and lead them to criticize, to judge, and to accuse and condemn one another, and to cherish selfishness and enmity. For these sins, God banished us from His presence; and all who follow our example will meet a similar fate." [41]

A Gripping Metaphor

This last stratagem, of getting the forces of righteousness to fight among themselves and thus lose the advantage of strength gained through unity was described by Ellen White in a vivid metaphor employed in a *Review and Herald* article in October 1893, written while she was serving in Australia.

An Adventist member, A. W. Stanton, had arisen, claiming that the Seventh-day Adventist Church had become spiritual Babylon, and alleged that Mrs. White herself supported this viewpoint. He quoted from her published writings frequently to support his erroneous view (one, incidentally, that we continue to hear even today). His tract, "The Loud Cry! Babylon Fallen!" published in 1893, created no small stir. [42]

Mrs. White took pen in hand to refute this slander against the remnant church—and the wrongful use of her writings in support of such heresy. She wrote a series of four articles for the *Review and Herald,* which were published weekly between August 22 and September 12, 1893, under the title "The Remnant Church Not Babylon." [43]

Then in an article published the next month, on October 17, she characterized this attack against the church with this memorable metaphor:

"When men arise, claiming to have a message from God, but instead of warring against principalities and powers, and the rulers of the darkness of this world, *they form a hollow square, and turn the weapons of warfare against the church militant,* be afraid of them. They do not bear the divine credentials.

"God has not given them any such burden of labor. They would tear down that which God would restore by the Laodicean message. He wounds only that He may heal, not cause to perish. The Lord lays upon no man a message that will discourage and dishearten the church. He reproves, He rebukes, He chastens; but it is only that He may restore and approve at last." [44]

Eight years later Ellen White employed this graphic metaphor again in the same periodical:

"Those who are fighting the battles for the Prince of life must point their weapons of warfare outward, and not form a hollow square and aim their missiles of destruction at those who are serving under the banner of Prince Immanuel. We have no time for wounding and tearing down one another." [45]

Tragically, there are still those in the church who continue this destructive practice to this very day!

In 1885 Mrs. White's attention was called to conditions that would obtain in the remnant church just before the return of Jesus—our time. She wrote in warning:

"The enemy is preparing for his last campaign against the church. . . . The worst enemies we have are those who are trying to destroy the influence of the watchmen upon the walls of Zion [an obvious reference to ministers and church leadership]. Satan works through agents. He is making an earnest effort here. He works according to a definite plan, and his agents act in concert. A line of unbelief stretches across the continent and is in communication with the church of God. Its influence has been exerted to undermine confidence in the work of the Spirit of God. . . . Be careful lest you be found aiding the enemy of God and man by spreading false reports and by criticisms and decided opposition." [46]

"Before" and "After"

The experience of the Christian church in apostolic times may give us insight into how this unfortunate spirit came about for them. In *The Acts of the Apostles* (1911), one of the last major literary works to come from the pen of Mrs. White, she discusses the galvanizing effect on the church of Pentecost, the "early rain" of the Holy Spirit:

"After the descent of the Holy Spirit, when the disciples went forth to proclaim a living Saviour, their one desire was the salvation of souls. They rejoiced in the sweetness of communion with saints. They were tender, thoughtful, self-denying, willing to make any sacrifice for the truth's sake. In their daily association with one another, they revealed the love that Christ had enjoined upon them. By unselfish words and deeds they strove to kindle this love in other hearts.

"Such a love the believers were ever to cherish. They were to go forward in willing obedience to the new commandment. So closely were they to be united with Christ that they would be enabled to fulfill all His requirements. Their lives were to magnify the power of a Saviour who could justify them by His righteousness." [47]

This was her description of the "before" stage. Would that that stage had continued indefinitely. Unfortunately, however, "a change" came "gradually": "The believers began to look for defects in others. Dwelling upon mistakes, giving place to unkind criticism, they lost sight of the Saviour and His love. They became more strict in regard to outward ceremonies, more particular about the theory than the practice of the faith. In their zeal to condemn others, they overlooked their own errors. They lost the brotherly love that Christ had enjoined, and, saddest of all, they were unconscious of their loss. They did not realize that happiness and joy were going out of their lives and that, having shut the love of God out of their hearts, they would soon walk in darkness." [48]

A Solution Projected

Only by a return to the love of Christ, Mrs. White declared, could Christians again attain to this wonderful unity (which is God's requirement as well as goal), if they are to finish the work the apostles began. [49]

And, with her gift for imagery, Ellen would speak of the "silken cord of love." Four times in her writings she employed this analogy. [50]

Martha Amadon, to whom we were earlier indebted for an

eyewitness account of the first major health reform vision of June 6, 1863, also tells us that an early vision in Battle Creek contained a message that emphasized the need for (and present lack of) Christian unity. As Mrs. Amadon tells the story:

"Sister White at one time arose to address the meeting concerning some who were too critical of each other because of differences of doctrine. While speaking she walked back and forth on the platform, earnestly appealing to the people, and pressing the question as to whether they had hold of the silken cord of love.

"Suddenly the sound went through the audience as if she dropped to the floor, but immediately it was apparent that she was wrapped in a vision of God's glory. What she saw was short and to the point, and sealed the truth of what she had been saying against the criticism prevalent.

"Her reproofs on such occasions might seem to have been severe, but she always ended with cheering encouragement to those who would obey the counsel of God." [51]

Ever her message was "My brother, my sister, be afraid to find fault, afraid to talk against your fellow workers. . . . Remember that those only will enter heaven who have overcome the temptation to think and speak evil." [52]

"Press Together!"

The appeal to her fellow Seventh-day Adventist church members to "press together!" appears 145 times in the published Ellen White writings. Typical is this statement, made at the 1891 General Conference session:

"Suppose we try daily to have our hearts united in the bonds of Christian love. 'I have somewhat against thee,' says the True Witness, 'because thou hast left thy first love' (Rev. 2:4). And He says, 'Except thou repent,' 'I will come unto thee quickly, and will remove thy candlestick out of his place' (Rev. 2:5). Why? Because in our separation from one another we are separated from Christ. We want to press together. Oh, how many times, when I have seemed to be in the presence of God and holy angels, I have heard the angel voice saying, 'Press together, press together, press together. Do not let Satan cast his hellish shadow between brethren. Press together; in unity there is strength.' " [53]

And the purpose of "press together" is that we may "press

forward," an expression Mrs. White used 130 times in her published writings, usually in the context of Paul's admonition:

"This one thing I do, forgetting those things which are behind, and reaching forth unto those things which are before, I press toward the mark for the prize of the high calling of God in Christ Jesus" (Phil. 3:13, 14).

What Unity Does *Not* Mean

Ellen White was very concerned that her hearers and readers not draw incorrect conclusions from her repeated calls to Christian unity within the church. There were at least three things that unity did *not* mean and she spelled them out very clearly. For example:

1. *Unity does not mean the total suspension of a Christian's critical faculties of the mind.* While it is eminently true that "this work is so important" that we cannot engage in criticism of others, [54] yet it is also true that there is a genuine, *legitimate* place for *constructive* criticism in the Christian walk.

Christians may—indeed, should—criticize:

a. *Themselves.* She frequently called Seventh-day Adventists to the task of arising and "closely" criticizing themselves, [55] particularly the various facets of the condition of one's spiritual health: temper, disposition, thoughts, words, inclinations, purposes, and deeds. [56]

b. *Ideas.* In Ellen White's day, as also in ours, many thoughts were published by Adventist writers that were, simply, wrong and incorrect. (And sometimes these errors of fact and idea even appeared in Seventh-day Adventist publications!) And while the word "discrimination" has come generally to have negative connotations in our day, yet we must not overlook the fact that a "discriminating" mind—one that distinguishes and differentiates between truth and error, right and wrong—is a very important, necessary acquirement.

On the heels of two major publishing debacles in the church— (1) the 10-part series of articles in the *Review and Herald* on inspiration/revelation in 1884, in which the then-General Conference president, George I. Butler, posited the ideas of differences of degrees in inspiration (Mrs. White would later come close to sarcasm when she refuted it: "I was shown that the Lord did not inspire the articles on inspiration . . ., neither did He approve their endorsement before our youth in the college"); [57] and (2) the pantheism flap created by Dr. John Harvey Kellogg's book *The Living Temple,* which deceived even top leaders in the church (and which Mrs. White characterized as the alpha of apostasy) [58] — Mrs. White wrote:

"If ever there was a time when the writings of everyone connected with our work should be closely criticized, it is now. The Lord has made known to me that His Word is to be studied, and as no such representations as those made in *Living Temple* are made in the Word, we are to reject them." [59]

c. *Human Plans.* Humans, including Christians, are not infallible; and Christian leaders, with the best of intentions, often make serious mistakes in their planning. While we are to preserve unity in every plan," [60] yet that unity is not to be the product of silence on the part of planning committees when unwise programs are proposed.

"In the multitude of counsellors there is safety" (Prov. 11:14; cf. Prov. 24:6). (Maybe not always wisdom — but certainly "safety"!)

In a testimony entitled "Our College" and addressed to the leaders of Battle Creek College in 1882, Mrs. White gave this pointed counsel:

" 'Counsel together' is the message which has been again and again repeated to me by the angel of God. By influencing one man's judgment, Satan may endeavor to control matters to suit himself. He may succeed in misleading the minds of two persons; but, when several consult together, there is more safety. *Every plan will be more closely criticized;* every advance move more carefully studied. Hence there will be less danger of precipitate, ill-advised moves, which would bring confusion, perplexity, and defeat. In union there is strength. In division there is weakness and defeat." [61]

2. *Unity does not mean uniformity.* Ellen White never envisaged that her call to unity would result in the production of a group of carbon-copy Seventh-day Adventists, all thinking exactly alike on all points, and speaking exactly the same words! [62]

Mrs. White often spoke of an elusive yet important quality of human personality and character that she characterized as "individuality." And she made it clear that true unity does not destroy a person's individuality [63] — nor should it!

"Unity in diversity" was a favorite motto, [64] and its importance and value were often stressed. [65] Indeed, "unity in diversity" is one of the hallmark characteristics of animate and inanimate nature [66] — no two snowflakes appear exactly the same under the microscope, and no human fingerprint ever matches that of another.

True unity does not destroy the personality of the Father and the Son, nor that of Christ and His followers. [67]

On this subject Mrs. White wrote:

"Let each worker remember that he has an individuality of his own, and this individuality is not to be submerged in any other human being. That individuality is to be sanctified, purified, refined, but it is not to be lost in the individuality of someone else." [68]

"No human being is to be the shadow of another human being. God's servants are to labor together in a unity that blends mind with mind." [69]

In a *Review and Herald* article in 1906 Mrs. White quoted the words of Christ on this subject. He said, she reported, "with earnest solemnity": "The church is made up of many minds, each of whom has an individuality. I gave My life in order that men and women, by divine grace, might blend in revealing a perfect pattern of My character, while at the same time retaining their individuality. No one has the right to disparage the individuality of any other human mind by uttering words of criticism or faultfinding and condemnation." [70]

And finally: "No person can sink his individuality in that of another, but we are all, as individuals, to be grafted into the one parent stock [Christ], and there is to be unity in diversity." [71]

3. *Unity does not mean silence against wrongdoing by church leaders.* Church workers or members are not to be "doormats," nor silently to "roll over and play dead," when wrongs are perpetrated in the church. Christian unity never covers this kind of silence, which can be interpreted as acquiescence or cowardice. (Someone once said with as much truth as irony, "Silence isn't always golden; sometimes it's only yellow!")

Sometime around 1909 there was in one of our conferences a serious problem that Ellen White met with her characteristic forthrightness. Apparently a number of members had lost confidence in the leadership of the field, and decided to withhold their tithe as an act of silent protest.

"But will you rob God because you think the management of the work is not right?" she inquired rhetorically. Then she laid down a four-point rule for the amelioration and redress of such difficulties:

"Make your complaint [1] plainly and [2] openly, [3] in the right spirit, [4] to the proper ones. Send in your petitions for things to be adjusted and set in order; but do not withdraw from the work of God, and prove unfaithful, because others are not doing right." [72]

Even church leaders!

Try Christ's "Recipe"

Ellen White's counsel was totally in harmony with the instruction of Jesus given in the eighteenth chapter of Matthew, where our Lord "shows us the principles upon which we are to act in *all* cases and under *all* circumstances." [73] She would amplify it further in these words: "Whatever the character of the offense may be, this does not change the plan God has made for the settlement of misunderstandings and personal injuries. Act out the spirit of Christ. Take the recipe God has provided, and carry it to the spiritually diseased [one]. Give him the remedy that will cure the disease of disaffection. Do your part to help him. Feel that it is a duty and privilege to do this, for the sake of the unity and peace of the church, which is very dear to the heart of Christ. He does not want any wound to remain unhealed on any member of His church." [74]

In Matthew 18 we find Christ's three-step "recipe" for problem-resolution:

First, if you have a grievance against your brother in the church, you are to go to him *"alone"* to discuss the fault (verse 15). Second, if he refuses to deal with you privately, then you are to take with you "one or two more, that in the mouth of two or three witnesses every word may be established" (verse 16). And, third, if he yet refuses to receive you, then you are to "tell it unto the church" (verse 17).

Notice, though, that you are not at liberty, *even now,* to proclaim it to the *world,* even after you have taken the third step. Said Mrs. White:

"Do not put him to shame by exposing his fault to others, nor bring dishonor upon Christ by making public the sin or error of one who bears His name. . . . We are *not* to *make it a matter of comment and criticism among ourselves; nor even after it is told to the church are we at liberty to repeat it to others.* A knowledge of the faults of Christians will be only a cause of stumbling to the unbelieving world; and by dwelling upon these things, we ourselves can receive only harm; for it is by beholding that we become changed. While we seek to correct the errors of a brother, the Spirit of Christ will lead us to *shield him,* as far as possible, *from the*

criticism of even his own brethren, and how much more from the
censure of the unbelieving world." [75]

How much untold damage has been done by Seventh-day Adventists with their own private printing presses who seek to parade the
evils—real and imagined—perpetrated by church members and
leaders before the church, and also the public at large, contrary to
this inspired commandment!

Even in Bible days there were some things that, though true,
were still not to be blazed abroad: "Tell it not in Gath, publish it not
in the streets of Askelon, lest the daughters of the Philistines rejoice,
lest the daughters of the uncircumcised triumph" (2 Sam. 1:20).

"Independent Ministries"

One cannot help wondering what counsel might come from the
prophet's pen were she alive today to behold the proliferation of the
so-called "independent ministries" within the Seventh-day Adventist
Church, particularly within North America.

Unquestionably some are doing a tremendous amount of good,
and are deserving of our offerings (if not our tithe); [76] but some of
these, unfortunately, focus upon the sins and shortcomings in the
church—especially those of its leadership—and forget that there
never has been a time in the history of the church when it had
perfect, infallible leaders. [77]

As long as Peter kept his eyes upon Jesus alone, he could even
walk on water! But when he took them off Jesus, and placed them
instead upon the other 11 members of the "General Conference
Committee" of that day, he not only sank like the stone for which he
was named; he very nearly lost his life (Matt. 14:28-32). [78]

As a matter of fact, there never was a time in the entire history of
the Christian church when it had perfect leaders—including now.
Indeed, when a church elects a man or woman to office, it gives that
person the right to make a mistake!

The first "General Conference Committee" of the apostolic
church gave Paul atrociously bad counsel (Acts 21:23, 24)—and it
resulted in the church being prematurely separated from his immediate presence and guidance which it so badly needed. [79]

Leaders do make mistakes (including the "leading" critics of
church leadership today). They always have; they always will. The
church rightly demands accountability of its leaders. But those

leaders need your prayers and *constructive* criticism—offered in a spirit of brotherly love and concern—far more than mean, spiteful, destructive criticism, which in the end accomplishes nothing positive and serves only to discourage the leader and to bring loss of confidence in leadership among the church membership at large.

And one somehow suspects that were she confronted with elements of this late-twentieth-century phenomenon in the midst of Adventism, Mrs. White might repeat the words she wrote in 1901:

"It is not according to God's order for His people to break up into separate parties. His ministers are not to follow their own impulses and feelings, doing as the human impulse dictates, as though they were not under God's authority. Every minister of God is to live in the strictest obedience to His Word, following the example of Christ. In his dealing with his fellow men he is to put on Christ." [80]

Good advice for laymen, as well as ministers, too!

To a layman in 1888 Ellen White wrote this urgent appeal:

"I call upon you, my brother, in the name of the Lord to unite with us, to close every door through which Satan would enter to cause strife and alienation among brethren. . . . There has been altogether too much moving in one's own independent judgment. . . .

"My brother, God's people are one body. God has a people whom He is leading, teaching, and guiding, that they may teach, and lead, and guide others. There will be among the remnant of these last days, as there was with ancient Israel, those who wish to move independently of the body, who are not willing to be subject to the body of the church, who are not willing to submit to advice or counsel, but ever bear in mind that God has a church upon the earth, and to that church God has delegated power. . . .

"Men will rise up against reproof; men will despise counsel; men will depart from the faith; men will apostatize; they will want to follow independent judgment. Just as surely as they do this, disaster and ruin of souls will be the result. In short, Satan will become their leader, and will work constantly to tear down the things which God is building up, and follow their own finite judgment and plans."

Speaking of "discordant elements" within the church who "feel fully capable to grasp in their arms large responsibilities, and to be an independent body under no control," Mrs. White warned, in language as strong as that which she had ever employed anywhere:

"It is a delusion of the enemy for anyone to feel that he can disconnect from the body, and work on an independent scale of his own, and think he is doing God's work. We are one body, and every member is to be united to the body. Not one is to be shut up to himself and live for himself. Men must be like-minded with God, pure, holy, sincere."[81]

In the "train of cars" vision dealing with modern spiritualism, which we considered in chapter 4, it seemed to Ellen White "that the whole world was on board" the train headed "with lightning speed" for destruction and "perdition."

"I asked the angel if there were none left. He had me look in an opposite direction, and I saw a little company traveling a narrow pathway. *All seemed to be firmly united, and bound together by the truth.*

"This little company looked care-worn, as though they had passed through severe trials and conflicts. And it seemed as if the sun had just appeared from behind the cloud, and shone upon their countenances, and caused them to look triumphant, as though their victories were nearly won." [82]

And in her last message to the General Conference session in 1913, Ellen White looked down to the very end of time, and encouragingly reported, *I saw God's people "moving into line."*

There is hope, at last, for God's remnant church!

Many critics of the remnant church today declare confidently that the SDA Church has become spiritual Babylon. Indeed, the message of many can be summarized in three points: 1. The church has become spiritual Babylon. 2. "Come out of her, my people," and come, join my offshoot movement. 3. And when you come, be sure you bring your money along with you!

Somehow the critics seem to have forgotten that it is the *sinners* who are sifted out of the remnant church—not the righteous!

"The church may appear as about to fall, *but it does not fall.* It remains, while the *sinners* in Zion will be sifted out—the chaff separated from the precious wheat." [83]

The righteous remnant stay with the ship, which in the end will sail triumphantly into the harbor with those who loyally have remained on board. *The righteous do not jump ship;* it is the *sinners* who will be *sifted out* as we near the end of the journey.

Secret in the Circle

In one sense the secret of the "line" is in the "circle." For it is only when one has been in the "circle" that he or she is properly prepared to take his or her place upon the "line."

The late Dr. Louis H. Evans, Sr., pastor, in the 1950s and 1960s, of Presbyterianism's largest congregation (Hollywood First), once told this story from his pulpit:

Napoleon had learned that discontent among his troops was rapidly ripening into open mutiny. Not a moment was to be lost.

"Order all the men, officers and soldiers, out on the parade ground," he instructed one of his generals. "Tell them to form a large circle, with arms outstretched, so that the fingertips of one will just touch the fingertips of another."

The order was executed, and then Napoleon himself appeared. He moved quickly to the exact center of the circle, and curtly gave the instruction: "When I say 'March,' each of you will take one step forward toward me. Do you understand?"

Then came the command, "March." As one, the army moved in unison. Then, again, "March." And again, and again, and again.

Napoleon noted with silent satisfaction the large circle of men progressively shrink into a smaller and still smaller circle. *As the soldiers came nearer and still nearer to their commander in chief, they also came nearer and still nearer to one another!*

Soon the circle had shrunk until the soldiers were standing, literally, shoulder to shoulder. As they had come nearer and nearer to their leader, they had come nearer and nearer to each other.

Napoleon surveyed his troops, looking intently for a moment into the face of each, and then abruptly turned upon his heel and left the parade ground. Back in command headquarters, he told his generals, "There is no revolt in France tonight."

Conclusion

As we in our circle come closer to *our* Commander, we will also simultaneously come closer to one another.

And if the *secret* of the "line" is in the "circle," then the *destiny* of the "line" is the "hollow square"—not the one Ellen White feared, where Christians turned their weapons against one another, but another "hollow square" that she beheld in vision, in which, after the

second coming of Jesus, the redeemed stood, to sing praises to the
God of their salvation! [84]

A parting thought:

"What sort of a church would my church be,
If every member were just like me?" [85]

Notes and References

[1] SDAE 493, 1214.

[2] *Ibid.,* p. 333. The school would be renamed, successively, as Washington Foreign Mission Seminary (1904), Washington Missionary College (1913), and Columbia Union College (1961).

[3] *Ibid.,* p. 502.

[4] *Ibid.*

[5] 5Bio 75, 241, 408; 6Bio 196.

[6] 6Bio 197.

[7] *Ibid.,* p. 387.

[8] GCB 1913, p. 34; republished in TM 513-515. (Italics supplied.)

[9] TM 514.

[10] *Ibid.,* p. 112; 1T 179-184; EW 269-273.

[11] 5T 136; GC 608; 2SM 368; Ev 301.

[12] See Roger W. Coon, "Ellen G. White and the Final 'Shaking' of Adventism" (unpublished lecture outline, Seventh-day Adventist Theological Seminary, Oct. 21, 1987) for a summary of the Ellen G. White position.

[13] For a typical sampling of EGW sentiments, see UL 369, 149, 141, 300, 153, 271, 71, 68, 104, and 76.

[14] 5BC 1148; MH 421, 422; 8T 269.

[15] 6T 236.

[16] DA 675, 676; MH 422; 8T 269, 239-243.

[17] E.g., see 5T 279.

[18] LHU 296.

[19] 3T 429, 434-459; 5T 477-490; TM 56.

[20] 8T 242, 243.

[21] 9T 180, 181, 197, 198.

[22] 9T 33.

[23] LS 302, 303; 6T 50; 7T 38; 9T 145, 193, 259.

[24] MM 48, 49.

[25] *Ibid.,* pp. 46, 47; 7T 111.

[26] 8T 46, 166, 167, 239-243; 1SM 199.

[27] 6T 235-242, 288-293; 8T 161, 162.

[28] 5T 553.

[29] CT 522.

[30] 7T 171.

[31] *Ibid.,* p. 156.

[32] 6T 235-242; 7T 131; 8T 166; 9T 136; Ev 104; MM 241.

[33] AH 37, 178, 310; 2T 698-700.

[34] TM 472. (This chapter, TM 472-475, was first published in 4SP 337-340.)

[35] TM 472, 473.

[36] *Ibid.,* pp. 473, 474.

[37] *Ibid.,* p. 474.

[38] *Ibid.*

[39] *Ibid.,* p. 475.

[40] 1SM 48.

[41] TM 475.

[42] See George E. Rice, "The Church: Voice of God?" *Ministry,* December 1987, pp. 4-6.

[43] Republished in TM 32-62.

[44] RH, Oct. 17, 1893. (Italics supplied.)

[45] *Ibid.,* Aug. 27, 1901.

[46] 5T 294, 295.

[47] AA 547, 548; cf. pp. 578-580; UL 358.

[48] *Ibid.,* p. 548; cf. p. 580; UL 358.

[49] 4T 65.

[50] RH, Apr. 5, 1887; ST, July 15, 1889; RH, Sept. 15, 1891; *Bible Echo,* Mar. 2, 1903.

[51] Cited in *Notebook Leaflets From the Elmshaven Library,* DF 105c.

[52] RH, Nov. 24, 1904.

[53] 2SM 374, 375, from SCB 1891, p. 260.

[54] Ms 148, 1899; in 1MR 371.

[55] 1MR 371; cf. 13MR 76; 19MR 206.

[56] 1SM 89.

[57] *Ibid.,* p. 23.

[58] *Ibid.,* pp. 197, 200, 203.

[59] CW 158.

[60] 6T 215.

[61] 5T 30. (Italics supplied.)

[62] CW 82.

[63] TM 29, 30.

[64] 5BC 1148; 6BC 1083, 1090.

[65] 1SM 21, 22.

[66] 5BC 1143.

[67] *Ibid.,* p. 1148; MH 422.

[68] GCB 1901, p. 462; cf. 2MCP 423.

[69] Letter 44, 1903, p. 2; cited in 2MCP 429.

[70] RH, Sept. 20, 1906; cf. 8T 212.

[71] 2MCP 426.

[72] 9T 249.

[73] UL 136. (Italics supplied.)

[74] *Ibid.,* p. 106.

[75] DA 440, 441. (Italics supplied.)

[76] See especially "Faithful Stewardship," 9T 245-252, and "The Spirit of Independence," pp. 257-261.

[77] Especially helpful is Joel Engelkemier's four-part series "Independent Ministries: Should We Support Them?" in *Adventist Review,* Dec. 7, 14, 21, and 28, 1989.

[78] DA 381, 382.

[79] AA 404, 405, 417.

[80] Letter 19, 1901, pp. 8, 9.

[81] Letter 33, 1888, pp. 8-10; cf. 1T 207, 417; 5T 291.

[82] 1SG 174, 175. (Italics supplied.)

[83] Letter 55, 1886, cited in 7BC 911. (Italics supplied.) For Ellen White's counsel to Dudley M. Canright, who contemplated leaving the SDA Church for another "ship" that seemed safer and more trustworthy, see 5T 571-573.

[84] GC 645, 646; cf. EW 16, 288; LS 66; 2SG 34; 1T 61.

[85] Cited in G. Campbell Morgan, *Great Chapters of the Bible* (New York: Fleming H. Revell Co., 1935), p. 208.

Selected Bibliography

Baker, Delbert W. *The Unknown Prophet.* Hagerstown, Md.: Review and Herald Pub. Assn., 1987.

Blackford, W. W. *War Years With Jeb Stuart.* New York: Scribner and Sons, 1946.

Canright, Dudley M. *Seventh-day Adventism Renounced.* Chicago: Fleming H. Revell Co., 1889.

Centennial Book of Spiritualism in America. Chicago: National Spiritualist Association of the United States of America, 1948.

Coon, Roger W. *A Gift of Light.* Washington, D.C.: Review and Herald Pub. Assn., 1983.

_____. *Heralds of New Light: Another Prophet to the Remnant?* Boise, Idaho: Pacific Press Pub. Assn., 1987.

Comprehensive Index to the Writings of Ellen G. White. Mountain View, Calif.: Pacific Press Pub. Assn., 1962.

Jemison, T. Housel. *A Prophet Among You.* Mountain View, Calif.: Pacific Press Pub. Assn., 1955.

Loughborough, J. N. *The Great Second Advent Movement.* Nashville: Southern Pub. Assn., 1905.

_____. *Rise and Progress of Seventh-day Adventists.* Battle Creek, Mich.: General Conference Association of Seventh-day Adventists, 1892.

Morison, Samuel Eliot, and Henry Steele Commager. *Growth of the American Republic, 1000-1865.* New York: Oxford University Press, 1942.

Nichol, Francis D. *Why I Believe in Mrs. E. G. White.* Washington,

D.C.: Review and Herald Pub. Assn., 1964.

Robinson, Dores Eugene. *The Story of Our Health Message*. Nashville: Southern Pub. Assn., 1955.

The Seventh-day Adventist Bible Commentary. Washington, D.C.: Review and Herald Pub. Assn., 1953-1957.

Seventh-day Adventist Encyclopedia. Washington, D.C.: Review and Herald Pub. Assn., 1976.

Spalding, Arthur W. *Origin and History of Seventh-day Adventists*. Washington, D.C.: Review and Herald Pub. Assn., 1961-1962.

Strand, Kenneth A., ed. *The Sabbath in Scripture and History*. Washington, D.C.: Review and Herald Pub. Assn., 1982.

White, Arthur L. *Ellen G. White: The Australian Years*. Washington, D.C.: Review and Herald Pub. Assn., 1983.

_____. *Ellen G. White: The Early Elmshaven Years*. Washington, D.C.: Review and Herald Pub. Assn., 1981.

_____. *Ellen G. White: The Early Years*. Washington, D.C.: Review and Herald Pub. Assn., 1985.

_____. *Ellen G. White: The Later Elmshaven Years*. Washington, D.C.: Review and Herald Pub. Assn., 1982.

_____. *Ellen G. White: The Lonely Years*. Washington, D.C.: Review and Herald Pub. Assn., 1984.

_____. *Ellen G. White: Messenger to the Remnant*. Washington, D.C.: Review and Herald Pub. Assn., 1969.

_____. *Ellen G. White: The Progressive Years*. Washington, D.C.: Review and Herald Pub. Assn., 1986.

White, Ellen G. *The Acts of the Apostles*. Mountain View, Calif.:

Pacific Press Pub. Assn., 1911.

_____. *The Adventist Home.* Nashville: Southern Pub. Assn., 1952.

_____. *Christ's Object Lessons.* Washington, D.C.: Review and Herald Pub. Assn., 1900.

_____. *Colporteur Ministry.* Mountain View, Calif.: Pacific Press Pub. Assn.,   1953.

_____. *Counsels on Diet and Foods.* Washington, D.C.: Review and Herald Pub. Assn., 1938.

_____. *Counsels on Health.* Mountain View, Calif.: Pacific Press Pub. Assn., 1923.

_____. *Counsels on Stewardship.* Washington, D.C.: Review and Herald Pub. Assn., 1940.

_____. *Counsels to Parents, Teachers, and Students.* Mountain View, Calif.: Pacific Press Pub. Assn., 1913.

_____. *Counsels to Writers and Editors.* Nashville: Southern Pub. Assn., 1946.

_____. *The Desire of Ages.* Mountain View, Calif.: Pacific Press Pub. Assn., 1898.

_____. *Early Writings.* Washington, D.C.: Review and Herald Pub. Assn., 1882.

_____. *Education.* Mountain View, Calif.: Pacific Press Pub. Assn., 1903.

_____. *Evangelism.* Washington, D.C.: Review and Herald Pub. Assn., 1946.

_____. *The Great Controversy.* Mountain View, Calif.: Pacific Press Pub. Assn., 1911.

_____. *Life Sketches of Ellen G. White.* Mountain View, Calif.: Pacific Press Pub. Assn., 1915.

_____. *Lift Him Up.* Hagerstown, Md.: Review and Herald Pub. Assn., 1988.

_____. *Manuscript Releases From the Files of the Letters and Manuscripts of Ellen G. White.* Washington, D.C.: Ellen G. White Estate.

_____. *Medical Ministry,* Mountain View, Calif.: Pacific Press Pub. Assn., 1932.

_____. *Mind, Character, and Personality.* Nashville: Southern Pub. Assn., 1977.

_____. *The Ministry of Healing.* Mountain View, Calif.: Pacific Press Pub. Assn., 1905.

_____. *My Life Today.* Washington, D.C.: Review and Herald Pub. Assn., 1952.

_____. *Patriarchs and Prophets.* Mountain View, Calif.: Pacific Press Pub. Assn., 1890.

_____. *Prophets and Kings.* Mountain View, Calif.: Pacific Press Pub. Assn., 1917.

_____. *Selected Messages.* Washington, D.C.: Review and Herald Pub. Assn., 1958, 1980.

_____. *Sons and Daughters of God.* Washington, D.C.: Review and Herald Pub. Assn., 1955.

_____. *The Spirit of Prophecy.* Battle Creek, Mich.: Seventh-day Adventist Pub. Assn., 1870-1884.

_____. *Spiritual Gifts.* Battle Creek, Mich.: Seventh-day Adventist Pub.

Assn., 1858-1864.

_____. *Steps to Christ.* Mountain View, Calif.: Pacific Press Pub. Assn., 1956.

_____. *Temperance.* Mountain View, Calif.: Pacific Press Pub. Assn., 1949.

_____. *Testimonies for the Church.* Mountain View, Calif.: Pacific Press Pub. Assn., 1855-1909.

_____. *Testimonies to Ministers.* Mountain View, Calif.: Pacific Press Pub. Assn., 1923.

_____. *The Upward Look.* Washington, D.C.: Review and Herald Pub. Assn., 1982.

_____. *Welfare Ministry.* Washington, D.C.: Review and Herald Pub. Assn., 1952.

White, James. *Life Incidents in Connection With the Great Advent Movement.* Battle Creek, Mich.: Seventh-day Adventist Pub. Assn., 1868.

Curriculum Vitae

Roger W. Coon, Ph.D., has served as an associate secretary of the Ellen G. White Estate, a service agency of the General Conference headquarters of the Seventh-day Adventist Church, in the Washington, D.C., suburb of Silver Spring, Maryland, since 1981. He also serves concurrently as adjunct professor of prophetic guidance at the Seventh-day Adventist Theological Seminary, Andrews University, Berrien Springs, Michigan.

Dr. Coon holds the B.A. in history and religion (La Sierra University, 1948), the M.A. in religion (Andrews University, 1959), and the Ph.D. in speech—rhetoric and public address (Michigan State University, 1969).

He entered the service of his church on June 11, 1948, and was formally ordained to its ministry on June 21, 1952. He has served on all six continents, variously as a preacher, pastor, evangelist, hospital chaplain, foreign missionary, and author, but chiefly as educator (34 of his 44 years of service have principally been spent in the college, university, and seminary classroom).

While serving in Nigeria (1952-1964), he was a cofounder of the Adventist Seminary of West Africa at Ilishan-Remo, teaching there during that institution's first four years of existence. From 1967 to 1978 he taught on the religion faculty of Pacific Union College, at Angwin, California.

Dr. Coon's writings have been translated into at least 10 languages, and articles from his pen have appeared frequently in the *Adventist Review, Signs of the Times, Ministry, Mission, Journal of Adventist Education, Adventist Heritage,* and *Dialogue,* among others.

Dr. Coon comes from a long line of preachers extending back more than 200 years into Scotland. In his father's family of eight sons, five were ordained Seventh-day Adventist ministers, a record not often matched within his denomination.

In 1948 he married the former E. Irene Strom, a certified public accountant who, in 1978, became the first woman to hold the post of auditor at church world headquarters. She subsequently became the first woman to audit an overseas division of the church.

The Coons have two grown children: Susan, a graduate registered nurse whose husband, Kevin McDaniel, is a minister in the Michigan Conference; and Donald, an electronics engineer.

Biographical sketches of Dr. Coon have been published in A. N. Marquis' *Who's Who in Religion* (first, second, and third editions) and in Jacques Cattell Press's *Directory of American Scholars* (sixth, seventh, and eighth editions).

The Complete Biography of Ellen G. White

Written by Arthur White, Ellen White's grandson, this "behind the scenes" look at the life of God's prophet contains material never before published. Little-known facts and quotations shed exciting insights into the development of the Seventh-day Adventist Church. You trace the early years of James and Ellen White, their courtship and marriage. In fascinating detail you watch health reform take root, church schools appear, the publishing work begin, missionaries sailing for distant lands, all from the viewpoint of Mrs. White.

Ride a mule train in Colorado, a buggy in New England, a steamboat on the Cumberland. Attend camp meetings under the canvas. Listen spellbound to debates at the 1888 Minneapolis session.

The six volumes are:
1. *The Early Years*, 1827-1862
2. *The Progressive Years*, 1862-1876
3. *The Lonely Years*, 1876-1891
4. *The Australian Years*, 1891-1900
5. *The Early Elmshaven Years*, 1900-1905
6. *The Later Elmshaven Years*, 1905-1915

Complete Ellen G. White biography set (six volumes with slipcover), US$99.95, Cdn$124.95. US$19.95, Cdn$24.95 each.

To order, call **1-800-765-6955** or write to ABC Mailing Service, P.O. Box 1119, Hagerstown, MD 21741. Send check or money order. Enclose applicable sales tax and 15 percent (minimum US$2.50) for postage and handling. Prices and availability subject to change without notice. Add 7 percent GST in Canada.

Essential Reading About and by Ellen White

Ellen G. White Manuscript Releases
By Ellen G. White. This set makes available a large segment of materials that were bypassed in the production of the standard Ellen White books. Ten volumes. Paper, US$8.95, Cdn$11.20 each.

Ellen G. White Sermons and Talks
By Ellen G. White. During the 70 years of her ministry Ellen White was called upon to speak in just about every imaginable situation. In this first volume of a new series we read her transcribed material as she originally gave it. Few of these messages have been previously published. Volume 1, 405 pages. Paper, US$8.95, Cdn$11.20.

Gift of Light
By Roger W. Coon. Introduce your non-Adventist friends as well as new church members to the gift of prophecy as exemplified in the life of Ellen White. Paper, 63 pages. US$1.35, Cdn$1.70.

The World of Ellen G. White
Gary Land, editor. This book takes you back in time to see the historical context of Ellen White's writings. Fourteen specialists examine specific areas of life in the 1800s. Together they have created a readable, accurate resource. Hardcover, 253 pages. US$16.95, Cdn$21.20.

The *Youth's Instructor* Articles
By Ellen G. White. Facsimile reproductions of Mrs. White's articles as they originally appeared in the *Youth's Instructor*. Hardcover, 640 pages. US$39.95, Cdn$49.95.

To order, call **1-800-765-6955** or write to ABC Mailing Service, P.O. Box 1119, Hagerstown, MD 21741. Send check or money order. Enclose applicable sales tax and 15 percent (minimum US$2.50) for postage and handling. Prices and availability subject to change without notice. Add 7 percent GST in Canada.